THE COUNTRY I LOVE BEST

Books by

OSWALD J. SMITH

Messages on Salvation
THE COUNTRY I LOVE BEST
THE MARVELS OF GRACE

Messages on the Deeper Life
THE MAN GOD USES

Messages on the Holy Spirit
THE ENDUEMENT OF POWER

Messages on Missions
THE CRY OF THE WORLD
TALES OF THE MISSION FIELD

Messages on Prophecy
PROPHECY—WHAT LIES AHEAD?

Messages on Revival and Evangelism
THE PASSION FOR SOULS

Messages on Special Subjects
THE CHALLENGE OF LIFE

Messages in Biography
THE LIVES OF BRAINERD AND FLETCHER
THE STORY OF MY LIFE

Messages for Young People
THE ADVENTURES OF ANDY MCGINNIS
THE STORIES OF THOMAS

Messages in Poetry
POEMS OF A LIFETIME

Messages in Hymns
OSWALD SMITH'S BEST SONGS
OSWALD SMITH'S FAVOURITES

Dr. Oswald J. Smith has reduced the number of his books. Above is a complete list of titles to be kept in circulation. All other titles have been discontinued. The author has taken out some chapters from the earlier editions of the books which will be continued under their former titles and substituted some chapters from the books no longer in print. In this way he has retained the most important material in a reduced number of books.

THE COUNTRY I LOVE BEST

AND HOW TO GET THERE

by

OSWALD J. SMITH, LITT.D.

Founder and Minister of Missions of the Peoples Church, Toronto

London
MARSHALL, MORGAN & SCOTT
Edinburgh

LONDON
MARSHALL, MORGAN AND SCOTT, LTD.
1–5 PORTPOOL LANE
HOLBORN, E.C.1

AUSTRALIA AND NEW ZEALAND
117–119 BURWOOD ROAD
MELBOURNE, E.13

SOUTH AFRICA
P.O. BOX 1720, STURK'S BUILDINGS
CAPE TOWN

CANADA
EVANGELICAL PUBLISHERS
241 YONGE STREET
TORONTO

THE PEOPLES CHURCH
374 SHEPPARD AVE. EAST
WILLOWDALE
ONTARIO

First edition 1934
Fourteenth edition (revised) 1965

MADE AND PRINTED IN GREAT BRITAIN BY PURNELL AND SONS, LTD.
PAULTON (SOMERSET) AND LONDON

CONTENTS

Not These, But Him

CHAPTER I

THE COUNTRY I LOVE BEST

DURING the past years of my life I have visited many different countries—seventy to be exact. To some of these countries I have gone again and again, to others but once. In very few have I felt at home. Always I have longed to return to Canada, my native land.

There are a few countries like those of North America, where it is possible to have any kind of climate and scenery desired; where there is an abundance of everything and but little to fear. To these countries thousands in Europe and other lands long to go. They yearn for freedom from want and from totalitarian governments.

But there is not a country in the world where any one of us would want to live for ever. Even in our own country there is so much sin, so much crime and lawlessness, so much drunkenness, debauchery and immorality, that we long for a better environment. War and bloodshed, poverty, sickness and death have brought us such sorrow and heartache that we feel like strangers and foreigners in a world that is not our home.

Let me tell you of a Country where there are no tears or heartaches, a Country where there is no sickness, pain or death. It is a Country free from war and bloodshed, and where no one is poverty-stricken. The people who live in this Country never get tired; they carry no burdens and they never grow old. No one ever says goodbye, for separations are unknown, and there are no disappointments.

In the Country of which I am speaking there is no sin, for no one ever does wrong. There are no accidents of any kind. You will travel for thousands of miles and never see a cemetery or meet a funeral procession. There are no undertakers and no morgues. You will never see crêpe on the doors, for no one ever dies. There they need no grave-diggers, and coffins are unknown. The clothes that are worn are bright and glistening, and no one dresses in mourning.

It is a Country where nothing ever spoils; the flowers never lose their fragrance and the leaves are always green. There are no thunder-storms, no erupting volcanoes, and no earthquakes. Upon those fair shores hurricanes and tidal waves never beat. There are no germs or fevers, no pestilences of any kind. The sun never shines and yet it is always light, for there is no night there. It is never too hot and never too cold. The temperature is exactly right. No clouds ever darken the sky, and harsh winds never blow.

There are no drunkards in this Country, for no one ever drinks. None are immoral, men as well as women are pure. There are no illegitimate babies. Prisons, jails and reformatories never darken the landscape. Doors have no locks and windows no bars, for thieves and robbers never enter there. No lustful books are read, and as for unclean pictures they are never seen. No taxes are paid and rents are unknown.

Yes, and let me tell you something else. There are no cripples to be seen anywhere. None are deformed or lame. Nor is anyone blind, deaf or dumb. Hence, homes for incurables have never been built, for all are healthy, all are well and strong. No beggars clutter the streets, for none are destitute and all have enough. Leprosy and cancer, palsy and tuberculosis are words that this Country has never heard. No asylums are there, for none are feeble-minded. Doctors are never needed and hospitals are unknown.

You ask me how I know all this? Have I been there? No, I have not yet had the privilege of visiting this wonderful Country of which I speak, but others have. And One, at least, who had lived there for a long, long time, has come and told me a great deal about it. He says it is called Heaven, and this is what He says about those who live there: "God shall wipe away all tears from their eyes; and there shall be no more death, neither sorrow, nor crying, neither shall there be any more pain" (Rev. 21: 3–4). He has now gone back again, for He was very lonely and often homesick when He was here.

But one of these days He is going to return, and meanwhile He has promised me a trip to His native Land. Ever since He told me about it I have been longing to go. And from what He says, I am sure I will never want to come back. I have decided to make His Country mine. In fact, I have already taken out my citizenship papers.

I cannot understand why everyone does not want to go. But they don't. Many, I find, like their own country better, and prefer to indulge in the sins to which they are accustomed, even though it means heartache and suffering, sorrow, disappointment and death. I cannot understand it, but it is true. I tell them about this Country and they only laugh. They do not believe me, and if they do, they don't care. I cannot persuade them to go with me. Some day the quota will be full and then it will be too late. How foolish they are!

This, then, is the Country about which I have been trying to tell you. Do you not now want to go? Do you know any other like it? Why not start to get ready for the journcy? It isn't difficult. Just open your heart to Jesus Christ, the Lord of the Country, and ask Him to come in and save you. Then you, too, will love it as I do. And one of these days, when the journey of life has ended, you will go to this wonderful Country and dwell there for ever more.

CHAPTER II

ONLY ONE WAY

A BANKER and a business man sat opposite each other in the manager's office. The business man, leaning forward, was talking most earnestly, when suddenly the other interrupted him.

"Ridiculous! Absurd! Foolishness!" And the proud banker curled his lip in scorn.

"But why?" inquired the one to whom he had spoken.

"Why? Do you, a thinking man, ask why? Such nonsense!" And he laughed in derision.

"Yes, sir," responded the other. "I ask you why?"

The face of the banker took on a scowl, and there was anger in his voice as he answered.

"Why? Do you mean to tell me that the death of Jesus Christ in my place on the cross is going to satisfy God? Away with such theories! If I am to be saved, I must accomplish it by my own efforts." And he stamped his foot with passion.

"Ah! I see," replied the other. "Now I know what is the trouble. You think you have a right to manufacture a way of your own, and so you reject and spurn the God-provided plan."

"What do you mean by that?" questioned the banker, with a mystified expression on his face.

"Now, listen! Suppose a man should come to you and say, 'Mr. Banker, I am in great need, and I want you to loan me some money.' Tell me, who would have the right to make the terms and conditions upon which the money was to be loaned, you as banker and owner, or the man in need?"

"Why, I would, of course. He would have to meet my conditions before he could get the money," replied the banker.

"Exactly. And that, sir, is your position. You are the poor, helpless sinner, lost and undone, and God is the great Banker. You are coming to Him for mercy and pardon. Will you tell me who has the right to make the terms and lay down the conditions upon which you may receive His salvation, remembering now that you are the man in need, and God the Banker?"

"Ah! I never saw it that way before," responded the banker in an astonished tone of voice. "Why, of course, I am not in a position to dictate terms. God has that right, and He alone."

"And yet you have been manufacturing a scheme of your own, forgetting that paupers do not dictate; they accept. And all the time God, the great Banker, has been offering you salvation according to His plan. Will you now abandon yours and accept His? Are you ready to meet God on His own terms?"

"God helping me, I will," replied the now humbled banker, as the new light broke upon his soul.

My friend, what about you? Have you too been manufacturing a way of your own? There are many who have.

Religion

A lot of people think that their *religion* saves them.

"Madam, how is it with your soul?" inquired a British nobleman of Madam Cherkoff of Russia.

"Sir," replied the indignant Countess, "that is a matter between my father confessor and God."

Was she not a member of the Greek Orthodox Church? Had she not paid large sums of money for its upkeep? Did she not believe and practise all its doctrines? Was she not faithful in her attendance on its services? Why then should she worry? It was no concern of hers; it was up to the Church to get her through.

Yes, my friend, and you, too, may be trusting in your church membership. But I want to tell you that religion cannot save. No religion, Protestant, Roman Catholic, Jewish, Greek Orthodox, Coptic, Mohammedan, Buddhist, Confucian, or any other, can save your soul. Only Jesus Christ can do that.

You may join as many churches as you like and still be lost. The church cannot save. You may be a Lutheran, a Presbyterian, a Methodist, a Baptist, an Episcopalian, or anything else, and yet perish. There is no salvation in the church. Salvation is in Christ.

Religion cannot impart life, and you must receive a new life in order to be saved.

Nicodemus was religious, but he wasn't saved. Jesus, therefore, said to him, "*Ye must be born again*". The Pharisee was religious, but he wasn't saved (Luke 7: 36–50). Cornelius was devoutly religious. He feared God, gave alms, prayed, fasted, was well thought of, and yet he, too, was lost and had to be saved (Acts 10: 22).

Paul was perhaps the most religious man of his day. His religion dated from his childhood. He spoke of himself as zealous for God. He had been circumcised and had kept the law blamelessly. And yet he was a sinner in the sight of God. He was lost though he knew it not. He, too, had to be saved for God's righteousness he did not have. He was religious, oh yes, a religious sinner. He called himself *the chief of sinners*.

Well, now, my friend, if religion could not save Paul and Cornelius, Nicodemus and the Pharisee, how then is it going to save you?

Have you ever heard of anyone as religious as John Wesley, the founder of Methodism? He was a minister of the Church of England and yet he himself says he was not converted.

He considered himself a Christian because he was religious, because he read his Bible, went to church, and said his prayers. He says he set apart an hour or two a day for religious retirement. He took communion and prayed for inward holiness. On Wednesdays and Fridays he fasted. He became a missionary to the Indians and preached the Gospel.

But Wesley was not saved. "Who shall convert me?" he cried. Oh, what a confession! His chief motive in becoming a missionary was, to quote his own words, "the hope of saving my own soul." What a tragedy! An Episcopalian clergyman, devoutly religious, and yet unsaved.

Are you, too, depending on your religious life for salvation? Then you are anchored to a false hope. You do not yet know Christ.

If religion can save, then why did Christ die? Calvary was unnecessary if religion, too, can save. No, my friend, there is but one Saviour, not religion, but Christ.

'Twas not the church that saved my soul,
Nor yet my life so free from sin;
'Twas Jesus Christ, the Lamb of God,
He rescued me, He took me in.

MORALITY

A great many people think they are saved because they live a good life. They rely on their morality to save them.

My friend, you might as well try to lift yourself by your own boot straps as to expect morality to save you.

If a moral, upright life can save, then why did Christ die? Of what value is His death? You don't need Him if you can save yourself.

If you could reach Heaven by your own efforts, you would cry out, "Look at me; I got in because of the wonderful life I lived. I was so good, so moral and upright, that God let me in. I didn't need a Saviour. Christ I ignored, I saved myself." But no, my friend, a thousand times, no! No one will ever talk like that, for no one can live a good enough life to satisfy God.

"*All our righteousnesses are as filthy rags*" (Isa. 64: 6), declares God. "*There is none righteous, no, not one*" (Rom. 3: 10). "*All have sinned,*" therefore, all need a Saviour.

In any case, if you are righteous, self-righteous, then Christ never came for you. "*I came not to call the righteous, but sinners to repentance*" (Luke 5: 32), He said. Are you righteous? Then, my friend, you do not need Christ.

"I am not an extortioner, nor am I unjust, I am not an adulterer," said the Pharisee. "I am not even a sinner like this publican. I am righteous." But the publican, with downcast eyes, smiting on his breast, cried, "*God, be merciful to me, a sinner.*" Jesus justified the publican but condemned the Pharisee (Luke 18: 9–14).

You know you are not righteous. Why, you wouldn't want your friends to know your thoughts. Do you think then you are fit to stand in the presence of a holy God?

You tell me there is no dust in this room? Let the sun in. Now look at that ray of light. No dust! Millions, millions of specks everywhere.

You say you are righteous. But wait a moment. Let the white light of God's holiness enter your heart. Now what? Corruption, vileness, pollution. In a word, sin.

Peter cried, "*I am a sinful man, O Lord.*" Job exclaimed, "*I am vile.*" Isaiah said, "*Woe is me!*" These men were the best, the most moral and upright of their day. But when they saw the Lord, they saw themselves.

Here is the testimony of a public executioner: "I have always been a God-fearing, religious person. I have endeavoured to lead an honest, moral life, and in my dealings with others, have tried to follow the Golden Rule. I have striven to be a good husband and a good father.

Wherever I may have failed, it has not been for lack of sincere effort."

Sounds good, doesn't it? But it is all wrong. It is all "I". He speaks of his own honesty and morality, and his efforts to adhere to the Golden Rule. But where is Christ? He is never even mentioned. He claims to be a religious man, not a saved man. There is no mention of the New Birth, no word about having accepted Christ. He seeks to be his own saviour and he bases his hope on his personal morality. What a false foundation. Yet there are millions like him.

And are you, too, going to stand on your own righteousness? My friend, you know you are not righteous. If you compare yourself with others, you may make a good showing; but when you measure yourself by the standards of God, how far short you fall! God demands a perfect righteousness and there is only One who has it. That one is Jesus Christ. If you are clothed in His righteousness you will be accepted; if not, you will be condemned. Your own is faulty; it will never avail.

You may do your best, but your best will never pass muster with God. But do you do your best? Have you ever done your best? You know you never have. Time and time again you could have done just a little better than you did, and if that be so then you did not do your best. No one does. Be honest now and face the facts. You are not doing the best you can, and you know it.

Then, my friend, you need Christ. Only the wedding garment of His righteousness will get you through. Like the prodigal, you must cast away your filthy rags, and let Him cover you with His spotless robe. Plead His merits, not yours.

Works

Multitudes think they are saved by their good works. They practise penance and self-denial. They give alms and say prayers. They visit the sick and imprisoned and perform numerous long pilgrimages and afflict their bodies. And thus they expect to get to Heaven.

They work "for" salvation, whereas God tells them to work "out" their salvation. It must become theirs first; then they can work it or live it out. The student must first enrol before he can work out his college career. You must first receive Christ and be saved; you must get salvation if you are to work it out.

What did the dying thief do to be saved? Work he could not, for his hands were nailed to a cross. He did nothing, yet Jesus saved him.

Man's plan of salvation emphasizes the word "do". God's speaks of "done". Man insists on doing something, paying something. He wants to merit salvation. God says it is done. There is nothing to do. Jesus did it all.

Salvation, my friend, is a gift. "*The gift of God is Eternal Life*" (Rom. 6: 23). What can you do to earn a gift? If you pay for it then it is not a gift. If you work for it you have a right to it, so then again, it is not a gift. A gift is free, and so is salvation.

What did the prodigal son pay? When you tell me how much he paid I will tell you how much you must pay. But you know he paid nothing, for he had nothing. He was bankrupt and so are you. Salvation, my friend, is without money and without price. It cannot be bought.

When I was in India I saw so-called holy men, working for salvation. "What are you lying on that bed of spikes for?" I might have asked. "To save my soul," would have been the answer. But why should they do what Christ did? Did He not suffer, bleed and die for them? Did He not atone for their sins? And is not God satisfied with the sacrifice of His Son? Why then should they, or you, seek to add to the finished work of Christ?

Hear now the Word of God. How clear it is! How emphatic!

"*For by grace are ye saved through faith; and that not*

of yourselves: it is the gift of God: not of works, lest any man should boast" (Eph. 2: 8–9).

"Not by works of righteousness which we have done" (Titus 3: 5).

"But to him that worketh not, but believeth on Him that justifieth the ungodly, his faith is counted for righteousness. God imputeth righteousness without works" (Rom. 4: 5, 6).

"Worketh not" and *"not of works"*. How definite! No work of yours, no deeds of merit, nothing that you can do will avail in the least. It is Christ and Christ alone who saves. Oh that you would come to Him, and rely on His finished work on Calvary, trust Him this moment and be saved.

'Twas not my works that saved my soul,
Nor yet my zeal, my prayers, my tears,
'Twas Jesus Christ, the Son of God,
He bore my sins, he calmed my fears.

Commandments

Some people think they are saved because they keep the commandments.

But Jesus said, *"None of you keepeth the law,"* and I would rather believe Him than you. You haven't kept the commandments, my friend, and what is more, you know it. At some time or other in your life you broke one of them. Now God says, *"Whosoever shall keep the whole law and yet offend in one point, he is guilty of all"* (Jas. 2: 10). One point, one sin, one commandment broken, and you have broken the law.

Then you are doomed. You are condemned. You are a sinner. You have transgressed, and you are guilty. Well, what are you going to do about it? "Oh," you say, "I am going to turn over a new leaf and live right. I will never again break the commandments." No? Don't be too sure. Frankly, I wouldn't trust you. But even if you could, what about the past? What about the commandment you broke? Will God overlook it?

Most certainly not. You must answer for every sin, that is, unless you will let Christ answer. He never broke the commandments. He was sinless. He kept the law perfectly. But because you did not, an atonement had to be made, a sacrifice offered. Now He, the Lamb of God, is my sacrifice. Why not let Him be yours, too?

Clean pages are fine and a clean life is ideal, but remember, you still have to reckon with the old pages with their blots of sin. God will not overlook them. They must be washed and washed clean. Every debt must be wiped out.

Suppose you run up a bill at the grocery store, and then one day, start to pay cash. Will that wipe out your debt, and cancel your bill? Why, certainly not. The debt remains until it is paid. Turn over a new leaf if you want to; start to keep the commandments if you can, but what about the ones you have broken?

But suppose someone walks in and pays your debt, then what? Oh, now you can begin anew. Pay from now on and all will be well. My friend, Christ paid your debt. He atoned for every commandment you broke, every sin you ever committed. Believe it, thank Him and go free.

It is as sensible to talk about keeping the law in order to be saved as it is to offer a patient in the sanatorium a book on the laws of health. He has a cancer and he needs a cure. You, too, are diseased. You have a sin cancer. You need someone who can take your disease and give you His health, not a book of laws. My friend, Christ did that. He took your sin, bore it in His own body on the cross, and now He offers you His life—eternal life.

Paul had a never-ending battle with the Judaizers of his day over the law. He called it "*the Jews' religion*" and turned from it to Christ. Listen to him:

"*Therefore by the deeds of the law there shall no flesh be justified. A man is justified by faith without the deeds of the law"* (Rom. 3: 20–28). *"If righteousness come by the law, then Christ is dead in vain"* (Gal. 2: 16–21).

'Twas not the law that saved my soul,
Nor yet the deeds of virtue done;
'Twas Jesus Christ, the Gift of God,
He bled, He died, my soul He won.

CHRIST THE ONLY SAVIOUR

My friend, thus far I have dealt with man's way—religion, morality, works, commandments—and proved it false. Now let me turn to God's way of salvation.

There is only One who can save, and that One—the resurrected, living Christ.

"I am the way; no man cometh unto the Father but by Me" (John 14: 6).

"I" Jesus Christ. There is no other. Not religion. Not morality. Nor good works. Christ, the Son of God, is the one and only Saviour.

He is "the Way". Not the way-show-er. No man can come to God but by Him. Neither by Moses, nor by Buddha. Not by Mohammed or Confucius. Nor by a priest, a minister or a pope. Only by Christ. Will you then let Him save you?

"Neither is there salvation in any other, for there is none other name under heaven, given among men, whereby we must be saved" (Acts 4: 12).

What a verse! There is no clearer statement in the Bible. Salvation is in no other. No other church. No other individual. Will you believe it? No other name—Roman Catholic, Greek Orthodox, Coptic, Protestant, Lutheran, Presbyterian, Methodist, Anglican, Baptist, Buddhist, Mohammedan, Confucianist. *"Thou shalt call His name Jesus for HE shall save."* Will you, then, turn from all others and trust Him, and Him alone? He only can save you.

"But will He save me?" you ask. *"Him that cometh to me I will in no wise cast out,"* are His own words (John 6: 37). He can cast you out or take you in. He says He will not cast you out. Then what will He do? He will take you in. Thank God for such a Saviour.

What You Must Do

Perhaps you think that because God has provided salvation there is nothing for you to do.

What a mistake! Can you not see that you must accept God's offer? The Bible says, *"Choose, Take, Receive."* Salvation has been provided, but you must accept it. I may offer you a glass of water, but you must take it. It is one thing for the doctor to prescribe medicine for you, but what good will it do unless you take it? You will have to receive Jesus Christ if you are ever to be saved.

Oh, my friend, take Christ. *"As many as received Him, to them gave He power to become the sons of God"* (John 1: 12). But only those who receive Him are His sons and daughters. No one has ever drifted into salvation. As a matter of fact, we cannot get anything without making a decision. Nor can we get salvation. We must act. A choice is absolutely necessary. Oh, then, receive Christ and receive Him now.

And remember, there is a difference between believing with the head and receiving in the heart. You believe the elevator can take you down. But you do not get down until you act on your belief and step into the elevator. You believe the train can take you to your destination. But you do not reach your destination until you act on your belief and enter the train. You believe Jesus can save you. But you are not saved until you act on your faith and trust Him.

This is the way The New English Bible states it: "Put your trust in the Lord Jesus, and you will be saved" (Acts 16: 31). Hence you must choose Christ, receive

Him, rely upon Him, give yourself to Him, put your trust in Him. It is faith that saves.

Now is the Time

Perhaps you know you must be saved, but you are putting it off for some other time.

There is no future with God. *"Now is the accepted time; behold, now is the day of salvation"* (2 Cor. 6: 2). God's time is "now". My friend, the hour has struck, the time is at hand. Now is the moment to decide. Tomorrow may be too late. *"Boast not thyself of tomorrow; for thou knowest not what a day may bring forth"* (Prov. 27: 1).

Whatever you do, don't procrastinate. Take Christ and take Him now. This moment Eternal Life may be yours. If Satan can persuade you to put it off, you may be lost forever. Come, then, accept Him now. *"Seek ye the Lord while He may be found, call ye upon Him while He is near"* (Isa. 55: 6). There is a time coming when He will not be found; therefore, receive Him, and receive Him—NOW.

CHAPTER III

MAN'S RUIN AND GOD'S REMEDY

IT WAS night. Another day had gone, and all was still. But what matter—it was always night in the cold, clammy dungeon where Barabbas lay. The sun now and then did manage to penetrate the inky blackness that ever reigned beneath the surface of the ground. But even then it could not be called light; it was only less dark.

And yet there was a difference, for this particular night was the night of doom for the murderer who awaited the execution of his awful sentence. It was the last night on earth for him, and well he knew it. His career was ended; his last crime committed.

Back in the darkest corner he crouched, deep in thought. A few more hours and all would be over. Ah, but would it? In the morning he would hear the footfall of the death warden as he came along the corridor. Then for a moment it would cease as he paused before the door of his dungeon. The great key would clank in the lock, the bolt fly back, and the heavy door swing slowly open. And then he would be dragged out, led to the fatal spot, and nailed to a cross. And there for hours, it might be, he would suffer the most excruciating agony that Roman ingenuity could devise, exposed to the public gaze of an indifferent populace; for he must pay the penalty of his crimes.

In the morning he *did* hear the steps of the jailer coming along the corridor. The key *was* placed in the lock. The bolt *did* fly back, and in another moment the great door was opened. And Barabbas still crouched in the darkest corner as before. But that was as far as his surmises of the night were realized.

"Barabbas, have you heard the Good News?" It was the warden's voice, jubilant and strong.

"What Good News?" responded the condemned man in a bitter tone. "All I know is that this is the day of my execution, and that you have come to lead me out to be crucified for my crimes." And he shrank farther back against the cold, wet wall.

"Ah! but you don't know," replied the warden in the same triumphant tone. "Listen, Barabbas, *Somebody died for you!"*

"Somebody died for me! What do you mean?"

"Come with me, and I will show you, Barabbas."

Through the door, along the corridor, past numerous cells, into the street, and beyond the wall of Jerusalem, they made their way, the jailer forging ahead, hurrying his dazed prisoner along. At last they paused.

"Do you see yonder cross?" he inquired, placing his hand on the shoulder of the other, and pointing to a hill some distance away.

The condemned man looked, but it was a few moments before he could comprehend the scene before him, so unaccustomed were his eyes to the light of day. But at last he saw and spoke:

"Yes, I see. There are three, are there not?"

"But do you see the centre one?"

"Yes."

"Well, Barabbas, that centre cross was made for you, and you were to have died on it this morning."

Slowly the light dawned and broke on his beclouded mind.

"Then—then that Man hanging on it is dying in my place, *for me*!"

"Yes, Barabbas, for you. Did I not tell you that *Somebody died for you*?"

"Can it be possible! *For me, dying for me; taking my place!* But yes, that cross was made for me, and I should have been hanging there now. And yet He is dying *in my stead.* He has taken my place. I can't understand it. I don't know why He did it. But He did, and I can't help but believe it. He is really and truly dying for me."

"Yes, Barabbas, for you."

And for you too, sinner friend. Jesus Christ the Son of God hung there that day for you as well as for Barabbas. *He took your place, died in your stead, became your Substitute, bore your sins, gave His life that you, a poor, lost and guilty sinner, might live.* What a Remedy for Man's Ruin!

There are four great truths in the Word of God that present Man's Ruin and God's Remedy. These truths I now want you to consider.

1. ALL MEN ARE LOST AND ON THEIR WAY TO PERDITION, BECAUSE ALL MEN ARE SINNERS IN THE SIGHT OF GOD.

The human race is rushing down a precipice toward destruction. God says: *"All we like sheep have gone astray; we have turned every one to his own way"* (Isa. 53: 6). It is because men are lost that Jesus Christ came to save them. The Bible says: *"The Son of man is come to seek and to save that which was lost"* (Luke 19: 10).

Now the reason men are lost is because they have sinned against God. I have sinned, you have sinned, all mankind has sinned. There is no one who has lived a sinless life. The Bible says: *"All have sinned, and come short of the glory of God"* (Rom. 3: 23). *"There is none righteous, no, not one"* (Rom. 3: 10). Hence, all are sinners in the sight of God.

You are not a sinner because you sin; you sin because you are a sinner. Your very nature is sinful. You were born in sin, you were shapen in iniquity. An apple tree is not an apple tree because it bears apples; it bears apples because it is an apple tree. You sin because you are already a sinner. You started going astray as soon as you came to the years of responsibility, and you have been going astray ever since.

What is the doom of sinners? *"The wicked is reserved to the day of destruction"* (Job 21: 30). *"Thou hast destroyed the wicked, thou hast put out their name for ever and ever"* (Ps. 9: 5). *"The wicked shall be turned into hell, and all the nations that forget God"* (Ps. 9: 17). In Psalm 37 we read these statements: *"Evil doers shall be cut off: the wicked shall perish: the transgressors shall be destroyed."*

In Malachi 4: 1 we read: *"All that do wickedly, shall be stubble: and the day that cometh shall burn them up, saith the Lord of hosts, that it shall leave them neither root nor branch."* Paul says they *"shall be punished with everlasting destruction"* (2 Thess. 1: 9). Finally, in Revelation 20: 15, we read: *"And whosoever was not found written in the book of life was cast into the lake of fire."*

So there is no hope for those out of Christ. The wicked are to perish. All whose names are not in the book of life will be lost, and lost forever. They have sinned against God, and now they are doomed.

My friend, will you be there? Are you to be numbered with the wicked? Then for you there is no hope. You are lost, and on your way to perdition. You may not believe it now but you will experience it hereafter. Therefore, trifle not. Your doom is sure. If you go on as you are, there is no hope. You are condemned for all eternity. Right now you are a lost soul, headed for destruction, for you have sinned against Almighty God. The lake of fire will be your doom, the second death your eternal destiny. You will be consigned to hell, along with all the nations that forget God.

You tell me you are not a great sinner. What difference

does it make? If you have sinned, you have sinned. No sin can enter Heaven. One transgression will bar you. The fact of the matter is, you are without excuse. You have transgressed the laws of God. You have broken His commandments. You have sinned against your own conscience. You know perfectly well that you are unfit to face a holy God.

If you have not yet accepted the Lord Jesus Christ as your own personal Saviour, then you are guilty of the greatest sin a man can commit, for you have spurned the love and mercy of God; you have refused His pardon; you have ignored His Son; you have turned your back on Jesus Christ. Therefore, my friend, there is no hope. You are lost and on your way to perdition because you are a sinner in the sight of God.

2. All Men are Doomed to Death, but Death is Followed by Judgment, from which there is no Escape.

The Bible says: *"The wages of sin is death"* (Rom. 6: 23). *"The soul that sinneth, it shall die"* (Ez. 18: 4). Death is therefore the outcome of sin. Death is the penalty. When I speak of death I am not referring to the death of the body, but to the death of the soul. I am not referring to the first death, but to the second death. If you, my friend, have only been born once, then you will have to die twice. It is only those who have been born twice who will die but once. What could be worse than eternal death? Are you willing to face it? Have you no fear in your heart? Do you not dread the thought of it? Would you not flee from it if you could? Think of it—death, your eternal doom.

The Bible says: *"It is appointed unto men once to die, but after this the judgment"* (Heb. 9: 27). Now the awful thing about physical death is the fact that it is followed by judgment, and from judgment there is no escape. A day is coming when every man out of Christ will have to meet God. Judgment is certain. Sooner or later there must be a judgment, a judgment over which Jesus Christ Himself will be the presiding judge. Today He is presented as a Saviour, but, if men will not have Him as a Saviour, then they will be compelled to face Him as a judge. God has committed all judgment to His Son (John 5: 22). Jesus, who Himself became man, will be the judge of man.

It is bad enough to be arraigned in an earthly court before an earthly judge, but what will it be to stand before the judge of all mankind and to know that the sentence He pronounces will be final? There can be no appeal to a higher court. His court is the highest of all. Moreover, His judgment will be absolutely righteous, because He knows the hearts of men. He will be impartial. No one will be able to hide anything from Him. He knows all that we have done, all that we have said, and all that we have thought. He knows our very motives.

All who do not know Christ will be arraigned before Him. *"It is a fearful thing to fall into the hands of the living God"* (Heb. 10: 31). The very thought of it ought to make us tremble. Our hearts should be filled with dread and alarm. Think of having all your thoughts exposed, not only before your friends, but before the entire universe. Think of having no answer, no excuse. Are you prepared to face it? Will you go into the presence of God unsaved? Would you have Him as your judge?

3. No Man Can be Saved by His Works of Righteousness, nor can the Church Deliver Him from His Doom.

Let me make it very clear, my friend, that you cannot be saved by your own works of righteousness. Paul, you remember, turned away from all reliance upon the good life he had lived, realizing that it could not save him. His word was, "For by grace are ye saved through faith; and that not of yourselves: it is the gift of God: not of works, lest any man should boast" (Eph. 2: 8–9).

Did you hear it? "Not of works." "Not by works of righteousness which we have done" (Titus 3: 5). Not what we do but what God has done. Works can never save. If they could you would have a right to boast. But God must have all the glory. "Salvation is of the Lord." You cannot do anything to save yourself. You might as well try to lift yourself by your own bootstraps. Man can never be his own saviour.

Live the most righteous life that you can live, perform as many good deeds as you can perform, obey the Golden Rule, if you will, observe the ten commandments most meticulously, do the very best you can—all will avail you nothing. Life is not imparted by good works. No deeds of merit, no pilgrimages, no prayers, no works of mercy, nothing that you can do will avail in the least. You cannot buy salvation. You cannot earn salvation. You cannot work for salvation. You cannot achieve salvation. Your own works can never save you.

Even the Church cannot deliver you from your doom. No church ever has, no church ever will. Religion cannot save you. I care not whether it be the Roman Catholic religion, the Protestant religion, the Mohammedan religion, Buddhism, Shintoism, Confucianism, Hinduism, or any other religion—there is no religion that can save. There is no church that can save. Therefore, it makes no difference what church you are a member of, so far as salvation is concerned, because your church cannot save you.

You may be a Jew, but Judaism cannot save you. You may be a Roman Catholic, but Roman Catholicism cannot save you. You may be a Protestant, but Protestantism cannot save you. There are no religions that can save. Man is not saved by religion, any more than he is saved by his own righteous acts. Paul was a religious man, but he was not saved by his religious life. Nicodemus was perhaps the most religious Jew that ever lived, but he was not saved by Judaism. Cornelius kept the law blamelessly, but the law could not save him.

You see, my friend, you have a disease. You have a sin cancer. Something has to be done about that cancer. It would not be sufficient to hand you a book of laws, rules and regulations, and ask you to read them. That would not cure you. It would make no difference what kind of a life you lived, the cancer would still be there. You might become the most religious man on the face of the earth, but the sin cancer would remain. Something, you see, has to be done about the cancer. You can do nothing about it yourself. Your righteousness, your religion, will have no effect on it whatever. Since you are a sinner in the sight of God, a cure must be found. You cannot be your own doctor, your own physician.

That is why I do not urge people to join the Church. I do not want to give them a false sense of security. Too many already are trusting in the Church for salvation. I know perfectly well that the Church cannot save them, and therefore I do not invite them to come forward to be baptised and join it. I would be deceiving them if I were to do that. I would be giving them the idea of being saved by uniting with the Church. That, my friend, is absolutely impossible. Church membership has nothing whatever to do with it. You may join all the churches in the world and still be lost, and lost eternally.

4. Salvation is the Gift of God, and it is Only by Christ, Through Faith, that Men Can Receive It.

God's salvation is a gift. If it is a gift it cannot be earned. There is no way to merit it. You cannot work for it. A gift has to be accepted as a gift. You must take God's salvation as you would take a Christmas present. All you can do is to receive it and thank Him for it. The price has already been paid, and it was enormous. God gave His only begotten Son. Jesus shed His life's blood on Calvary's Cross. Jesus bore the penalty for sin. That penalty was death. Jesus gave His life. He made a full and complete atonement, an atonement that satisfied divine justice and met the needs of man. Jesus paid it all.

"The gift of God is eternal life through Jesus Christ our Lord" (Rom. 6: 23). *"God hath given to us eternal life, and this life is in His Son. He that hath the Son hath life, and he that hath not the Son of God hath not life"* (1 John 5: 11, 12). Therefore, if you will accept God's salvation as a gift by accepting Jesus Christ, you will be saved. You see, there is hope for you. You do not have to perish. You may be doomed, but you can escape; that is, if you will accept the mercy of God as it is offered in His Son, Jesus Christ.

Suppose I owed a large bill which I could not pay. Either someone else would have to pay it for me, or I would have to take the consequences. That is man's situation before God. He owed a debt he could not pay. Jesus Christ stepped in and paid the debt. If man will accept the provision that Christ has made, he may go free. The Bible says, *"The Lord hath laid upon Him the iniquity of us all"* (Isa. 53: 6). Christ has become his substitute. An atonement has been made. God can now offer salvation without money and without price.

Now let me make it perfectly clear that the only way you can accept Christ is by faith. Again and again God offers you salvation by faith in Christ. It is not a head belief, it is a heart belief. It is best expressed by the word trust. All the intellectual faith in the world will never save you. You must trust Christ as you trust an elevator, as you would trust a train, as you would trust a bank. It must be a practical faith. You must rely wholly upon Him for time and eternity. In other words, you must receive Him. The Bible says: *"As many as received Him, to them gave He power to become the sons of God"* (John 1: 12). "Put your trust in the Lord Jesus, and you will be saved" (Acts 16: 31—N.E.B.).

Your intellect, you see, has nothing whatever to do with it. It doesn't matter what you think or what you believe; all that matters is: Have you received the Lord Jesus Christ as your Saviour, have you trusted Him, have you put your faith in the Son of God, and are you now His child? You are saved by a Person.

It is like a drowning man—he has to have a rescuer. Someone must dive in and save him. What has that to do with your own righteous living? What has that to do with your church membership? You have to be saved by a person and that Person the Lord Jesus Christ. If Christ has not saved you, then you are not saved at all, for no one else can. He is the one and only Saviour. That is why God says, *"He that hath the Son hath life; and he that hath not the Son of God hath not life"* (1 John 5: 12). Eternal life is in Christ. He then must become your Saviour.

In Revelation 3: 20 it says: *"Behold, I stand at the door, and knock: if any man hear my voice, and open the door, I will come in."* You see, Christ stands on the outside of the door of your heart. The knob is on the inside. He will not force His way in. You will have to open the door and let Him in. But the moment you do, He will come in and you will be saved. Christ must somehow get into your heart, into your life. When that happens you are born again, born of the Spirit, born from above. You have passed from death unto life. You have received Jesus Christ as your own personal Saviour, and, trusting Him, you are saved for time and eternity.

Peter was very blunt. He exclaimed, *"Neither is there salvation in any other; for there is none other name under heaven given among men, whereby we must be saved"* (Acts 4: 12). That, my friend, rules out all others. All other so-called saviours. All other names. It rules out Buddhism, Shintoism, Mohammedanism, Confucianism,

Hinduism, shrines and idols. They must all be renounced. Not one of them can save. There must be a clean break and no compromise of any kind. All man-made religion must be utterly forsaken.

The founders and leaders of all such religions are dead. How then can they save? But our Saviour, Jesus Christ, is alive and alive forevermore. *"He ever liveth"* (Hebrews 7: 25). A dead Christ could not save. Jesus died but He rose again and He lives today. It is the resurrected Christ who saves. The tomb is empty.

Jesus was dogmatic. He said, *"I am the way . . . no man cometh unto the Father, but by me"* (John 14: 6). There is no other way. All ways do not lead to God, only one way, and Jesus says He is the Way. Not Mohammed, Confucius, Buddha, the Pope, the Emperor, but Christ. He is the one and only Way. There is no other. Not religion, not the Church, not baptism or confirmation, not good works or a good life, but Jesus Christ Himself. There is no way to God but Christ. Not Judaism, Protestantism, Lutherism, Episcopalianism, Catholicism, but Christ. *"I am the way."*

Oh then, my friend, trust Jesus, the Resurrected Living Jesus, God's only begotten Son. Receive Him. Put your faith in Him. Turn from all else. Rely only on Him, for He alone can save you. It takes a Living Saviour to save.

Have I made it plain? Then what about you? Are you saved or are you lost? Is it Man's Ruin or God's Remedy? If you are lost then will you not right now accept Jesus Christ, God's Remedy for Man's Ruin, as your own personal Saviour? "Put your trust in the Lord Jesus, and you will be saved." Will you do it? Do it and do it—NOW.

CHAPTER IV

THE QUESTION THAT SETTLES DESTINY

THERE was a young man one time who lived in the Western States. He had never done anything very wrong. But one day he was playing a game of cards and he lost his temper. Picking up a revolver, he shot his opponent and killed him. He was arrested and tried. Finally he was sentenced to hang.

But because of the wonderful life he had previously lived, his relatives and friends got up a petition for him. It seemed as though everyone wanted to sign it. Before long other towns and villages heard about it, and people all over the state eagerly signed the petition.

At last it was taken to the governor, who was a Christian, and tears came to his eyes as he looked at the large baskets filled with petitions. He decided to pardon the young man, and so, writing out the pardon, he put it in his pocket, and then, dressed in the garb of a clergyman, he made his way to the prison.

As he approached the death cell the young man sprang to the bars. "Get out of here," he cried. "I don't want to see you. I have had seven of your kind already. I had enough religion at home." "But," said the governor, "wait a moment, young man, I have something for you. Let me talk to you."

"Listen," exclaimed the young man, in anger, "if you don't get out of here at once, I'll call the guard and have you put out." "But, young man," exclaimed the governor, "I have news for you, the very best. Won't you let me tell you about it?" "You heard what I said," responded the young man, "and if you don't leave immediately I'll call the warden." "Very well," replied the governor, and with a sad heart he turned away and left.

In a few moments the warden approached. "Well, young man," he said, "I see you have had a visit from the governor." "What!" cried the young man. "Was that man dressed in the garb of a clergyman the governor?" "He was," replied the warden, "and he had a pardon in his pocket for you, but you wouldn't even listen to him."

"Get me pen, get me ink, get me paper," cried the young man. And sitting down he wrote, "Dear Governor, I owe you an apology. I am sorry for the way I treated you . . ." and so on. The governor received the letter, turned it over and wrote on the back, "No longer interested in this case."

The day came for the young man to die. "Is there anything you want to say before you die?" he was asked. "Yes," said the young man. "Tell the young men of America that I am not dying for my crime. I am not dying because I am a murderer. The governor pardoned me. I could have lived. Tell them that I am dying because I would not listen to the governor's offer."

My friend, if you are lost it will not be because of your sins, it will be because you will not accept the pardon that God offers you through His Son. For if you refuse Jesus Christ, what can God do? You are turning down your one and only hope of salvation.

In 1892 Wilson and Porter were sentenced to be hanged for robbing the U.S. mails. Porter was executed but Wilson pardoned. He refused his pardon and Chief Justice John Marshall of the Supreme Court handed down this decision:

"A pardon is a deed, to the validity of which delivery is essential, and delivery is not complete without acceptance. It may then be rejected by the person to whom it is tendered; and if it is rejected, we have discovered no power in a Court to force it upon him."

The responsibility, you see, rests upon you. If you will

not accept God's pardon, He will not force it upon you. "How shall we escape, if we neglect (or reject) so great salvation?" (Heb. 2:3).

Pilate

Pilate put it this way: "What shall I do then with Jesus which is called Christ?" (Matt. 27: 22). That is the Question that Settles Destiny.

Again and again he had tried to save Jesus. Then in despair he brought out Barabbas, and, standing Jesus and Barabbas side by side, he turned to the multitude and asked the question, "Whether of the twain will ye that I release unto you, Jesus or Barabbas?"

Incited by the priests, they answered, "Barabbas! Barabbas!" Then came Pilate's question, "What shall I do then with Jesus? You have chosen Barabbas, Jesus is still on my hands. I have yet to deal with Him. I must do something. What shall I do?"

Pilate, you remember, tried to shift the responsibility. First of all he told the Jews to take Him and judge Him, but they answered: "We are not allowed to put a man to death and this man is worthy of death."

Then hearing that He was of Herod's jurisdiction, he sent Him to Herod. But Herod quickly sent him back.

Finally, in desperation, he called for a basin of water and washed his hands before the multitude, as if to say: "I am no longer responsible and I wash my hands of the whole matter."

There is a legend told of Pilate. He is in the lowest depths of Hades and he is washing his hands in a basin of water. Every now and again he lifts them up and looks at them, but they are covered with blood. Again he plunges them into the basin of water and vigorously washes them in an effort to wash off the stains. Once more he holds them up before him, but still they are crimson with blood. Then in a voice of anguish he cries out, "Will they never be clean? Will they never be clean?" No, Pilate, your hands will never be clean, for they are stained with the blood of the Son of God.

Suppose I could summon Pilate to me now. Suppose I could command him to stand by my side on this platform, I wonder what he would say? For Pilate is alive, remember. Pilate has been alive for all these centuries. For more than nineteen hundred years he has been thinking of what he did when Jesus stood before him. He never can forget. He always will remember. His brain is still active. What, I ask, would he say?

Ah, but for Pilate it is too late. It would make no difference, he could never be saved. He has made his eternal decision. But for you there is still time. You are yet in the body. You may still decide what you are going to do with Jesus, and your whole eternity depends on your decision.

Only Two Alternatives

There are only two alternatives. You must either accept Jesus Christ or reject Him. "But," you say, "I can be neutral. I do not have to take sides. I am not going to accept Him, but at the same time I am not going to reject Him."

Listen, I have a gift for you in my pocket, but I do not tell you anything about it. Hence, you can be neutral. The moment, however, that I take it out of my pocket and offer it to you, you are bound to make a decision. You can no longer remain neutral.

Before you ever heard anything about the Lord Jesus Christ, you could be neutral. But the very moment He was offered you had to make a decision. And from that day to this, you have never been neutral, nor can you ever be neutral again. Every time you hear the invitation you will make a decision.

If tonight you do not accept Jesus Christ, then you reject Him. It is either one or the other. You may remain in your seat and make no move whatever. But by that very act you show that for tonight at least you reject Him. Which is it to be? Are you going to reject Him again, or will you right now accept Him as your own personal Saviour? It is for you to decide.

God's Basis of Judgment

May I point out that God will have to judge you on the basis of your last decision. Suppose, for instance, you decide tonight to reject Jesus Christ, but at the same time you make up your mind that next Sunday night you will reverse your decision and accept Him. Now suppose you die before next Sunday night. Think you God will judge you on the basis of what you might have done had you lived? Most certainly not. He will have to judge you on the basis of what you did do.

The question on the Judgment Day will not be a *sin* question; it will be a *Son* question. It will be a question concerning your relationship to Jesus Christ. "What did you do with my Son?" God will ask. "Well, Lord," you will answer, "I was always a religious man. I went to church——" "Wait a moment," God will interrupt. "I never asked you anything about your religious life. I asked you one simple question. What did you do with my Son?"

"Well, Lord," you will continue, "I always lived a good life. I never did anything wrong. I——" "Wait a moment," God will say again, "I never asked you anything about the life you lived. I asked you one simple question. What did you do with my Son?"

"Well, Lord," you will respond, "I always thought your Son was a good man. As a matter of fact, I thought He was the best——" "I never asked you what you thought about my Son," God will interrupt again. "I asked you what you *did* with my Son. Now tell me, did you accept Him or did you reject Him? What did you do with Him?"

And you will be silent. You will have no answer, for you did nothing. You just neglected Him. Hence, you will be lost, not because of what you did, but because of what you failed to do.

Why Will Men Perish?

Why, then, will men perish? If men are not going to perish because of their sins, then why will they perish?

There was once a young lady who was very ill. She was a member of the church. One day she passed into a trance and in her trance she dreamed that she had died, and that she was standing before the angel Gabriel at the gate of Heaven, while the angel was turning over the pages of the Book of Life.

After a while, with a sad expression on his face, he looked up. "Young lady," he said, "your name isn't here." "What!" she exclaimed. "My name isn't there? It must be. Look again." Once more he scanned the pages, but finally looking up he said again, "Young lady, your name isn't here."

"Why," she cried, "what have I done, what have I done, that my name isn't there?" "Young lady," replied the angel Gabriel, "it is not because of what you *have done* that your name isn't here. It is because of what *you have not done*. You have neglected the great salvation."

With that she awoke and, ill though she was, she crawled out of bed, knelt at her bedside and there and then for the first time in her life, opened her heart to Jesus Christ and received Him as her own personal Saviour.

Why will men perish? Let God answer. Look at John 3: 18: "He that believeth not is condemned already." Why? Because he has not joined the church? Because he has sinned? Is that what it says? It does not. This is the way it reads: "He that believeth not is condemned already, because *he hath not believed . . .*" That, my friend, is the only reason men are condemned.

You will never be lost because you are a murderer. God can forgive a murderer. You will never perish because you are a drunkard or a thief. God can forgive drunkards and thieves. But there is one sin God cannot forgive, and that is the final rejection of His Son. If you refuse to receive Jesus Christ as your Saviour there is no hope for you, for God has no other plan.

A Kind-Hearted Man

You say it is not fair. You think of your good life and you cannot understand why you should be condemned just because you have not accepted Jesus Christ.

Listen, you have a kind-hearted man here in your city. He is kind to his parents, kind to his children, and kind to his friends and neighbours. But he takes his wife whom he has promised to love and cherish, and he abuses her shamefully and then leaves her lying half-dead on the floor. He is arrested. Witnesses are called, one hundred of them. They all give the same testimony. "This man," they say, "was kind. He was kind to his father and mother, his sons and daughters. He was kind to his neighbours and friends."

Finally, the judge addresses the court. "I am not dealing with this man on the basis of his treatment of others," he says, "I am judging him on one point and one point alone: his treatment of his wife. Now tell me, was he kind to his wife?" There is not a witness. Finally he is condemned and sentenced. Yes, and rightly so, even though his crime was committed against only one person.

My friend, do you think you can be kind to the people of this world, and then be unkind to God's Son and not be guilty? Never. It doesn't matter what kind of life you live or how you treat your fellow men. If you ignore and neglect Jesus Christ, God will hold you accountable. You cannot ill-treat His Son and escape.

Nineteen hundred years ago God gave His Son for you. Jesus Christ bore your sins in His own body on the tree. He died that you might live. Now God offers you salvation without money and without price, and tells you to receive His Son as your Saviour. If you refuse, what can He do but condemn you? Everything, therefore, depends upon your relationship to Jesus Christ.

Your life may be most exemplary. Possibly no one could bring a charge against your character. To your friends and neighbours you have been most kind. But you have ill-treated the Son of God. Again and again you have rejected His offers of mercy. Outside the door of your heart He has stood for years, but never yet have you been kind enough to let Him in.

Now what do you suppose God will say when you stand in His presence? Will your kindness to your fellow-men make up for your unkindness to Jesus Christ? Not if the Bible is the Word of God. Hence, it is fair, after all. Your other sins fade into insignificance in the face of this, your greatest of all crimes, the rejection of the Son of God.

Your Enemy

Do you still insist that God is unjust, that He has no right to condemn you for refusing to accept Jesus Christ as your Saviour?

Listen! You have an enemy. Every injury that lay in his power he has done you. He hates the sight of you, and curses the ground you walk on. Through him your home has been broken up and your family life ruined.

But there comes a day when he is hungry, starving to death. You hear of it, and in the kindness of your heart you search him out and persuade him to come to your home. Food is brought and placed before him, abundance of it, and he is urged to eat. But all the urging goes unheeded. By the side of the table loaded with life-giving food he sits, but he never raises a hand to take. Finally he sinks down and expires at your feet.

Now tell me, why did he die? What more could have been done? Nothing! He died because he would not live. Life was within his reach, but he chose death. Yea, more, he was urged to take and eat, but he would not. Hence, he died. And how could it have been otherwise?

Without Jesus

Let me change Pilate's question somewhat. Let me put it this way: "What shall I do *without* Jesus?"

What are you going to do without Jesus in the hour of death? Are you willing to face your last enemy alone? I wouldn't take all the millions of this world and go through the valley of death without Jesus Christ.

What are you going to do without Jesus on the Judgment Day? Would you stand before God alone? I wouldn't take earth's millions and face God without an advocate. I want someone to stand by my side and plead my case.

What are you going to do without Jesus in Eternity? One thousand years from tonight you will be somewhere. Ah yes, but where? And that will only be the beginning. Can you face the countless ages of Eternity without Jesus?

What will you do without Jesus in the hour of sorrow? Perhaps you are young. You have never been bereaved. Rest assured that before many years have passed tragedy will strike. Do you think you can bear sorrow alone?

The Two Indian Mothers

When I was nineteen years of age, I was a missionary to the Indians. I lived alone on an Indian reserve up near Alaska.

One day a little Indian baby died. It was buried in a grave on the shores of the Pacific, under the primeval trees of the great forest. The mother watched as the earth was thrown in. Suddenly she put her two hands to her head and began tearing out her hair in great handfuls, until her head was a mass of blood. Then returning through the village street, she wailed so that she could be heard half a mile away.

While I was there another little Indian baby died. I took the little body in my arms and led the way through the forest along the Indian trail to the shore of the Pacific, the Indians following in single file as Indians do. There in the rocky soil we dug another little grave and placed the body in it. As the earth was thrown in, the Indian mother stood by the side of the grave weeping, not wailing aloud and tearing her hair, but just weeping silently. And when it was all over she returned to her little humble shack weeping to herself.

Why the great difference? Both mothers had lost a baby. Both mothers loved their babies as much as you mothers love your babies. But one was able to bear her grief while the other was not. Why, I ask, the difference?

The first mother was a heathen mother. She did not know Jesus Christ. She looked into the face of her little one, and she cried, "I'll never see my baby again." No wonder she wailed aloud. No wonder she tore out her hair.

The other mother was a Christian. She knew Jesus Christ, and the glad hope of the resurrection throbbed in her heart. "He shall not return to me," she said, "but I shall go to him." She knew that the great Shepherd of the sheep would take her little lamb in His arms and keep it until He could hand it back to her, and that then she would have it for all Eternity.

It is always so. Every time I conduct a funeral service it is the same. Those who know Jesus Christ are able to bear their grief because of the hope of reunion by and by.

Those who do not know Him cannot face such sorrow. They almost go wild with grief. I do not know how you can face your sorrow without Jesus Christ.

Your Decision

"What shall I do then with Jesus which is called Christ?" No, my friend, that is not the question. The question then will be: "What will Jesus do with me?" The question now is: "What shall I do with Him?" What Jesus Christ does with you *then* will depend upon what you do with Him *now*.

What shall I do? You will have to do something. A decision must be made.

What shall I do? It is an individual decision. No one can decide for you. You will have to decide for yourself.

What shall I do then with *Jesus*? It doesn't matter very much what church you join or how you have been baptised. All that matters *first* is your relationship to Jesus Christ. What are you going to do with *Him*?

What shall I *do*? It is not, What shall *I believe*? It is, What shall I *DO*? It is not an intellectual question at all. It has to do, not with your head, but with your heart, your will. Never mind what you believe; decide what you are going to do. Will you accept or will you reject? Your decision will determine your eternal destiny.

Therefore, I beg you to decide and decide now. Do not put it off until tomorrow. Settle it tonight. Tomorrow may be too late. "Now is the accepted time; behold, now is the day of salvation" (2 Cor. 6: 2). What then will be your answer? If you accept Him you will be saved. If you reject Him you will be lost. Oh, then, accept Him and accept Him—NOW.

CHAPTER V

WHAT DOES IT MEAN TO BELIEVE?

THERE was a time in my life when I did not know whether I was saved or whether I was lost. I remember working for the Massey-Harris Company in Toronto, and carrying messages from one department to another. As I walked along the underground corridors of that great firm I was not interested in the message I was carrying. I was asking myself just one question: "Am I saved or am I lost?"

After a while I left the Massey-Harris Company and was sent by the Upper Canada Bible Society to sell Bibles in Muskoka, the American playground of Canada. But as I trudged along the dusty country roads with my pack of Bibles, I did not see the beautiful lakes and rivers, the magnificent flowers or the evergreens. Nor did I hear the singing of the birds. I was still asking myself the same question, "Lord, am I saved or am I lost? If I am lost let me know it in order that I may get saved, and if I am saved let me know it in order that I may rejoice in Thy salvation." But my summer's work ended and I returned to Toronto, still not knowing whether I was bound for Heaven or for Hell.

The first Sunday I got back I attended Chalmer's Presbyterian Church, and as I sat on the east side of the gallery I bowed my head and prayed that the minister would that night preach on saving faith and thus solve my problem. At last Dr. MacPherson stepped into the pulpit and the service commenced. And that night he did preach on faith. I listened with both ears and watched with both eyes, but at the close of the service, with hundreds of others, I got up and went out into the darkness of the night, still not knowing whether I was saved or whether I was lost.

Why? Was it because Dr. MacPherson had not preached the Gospel? Most assuredly not. He did preach the Gospel. Again and again he cried out: "Believe on the Lord Jesus Christ, and thou shalt be saved." What then was the matter? Let me tell you. Never once in the course of his address did he stop to tell us what he meant by the word "believe", and that was my trouble. I knew that I had to believe, but I had always believed. There never had been a time when I did not believe. From the days of my earliest childhood I believed as much as I believe today, and yet I did not know whether I was a Christian or not.

You see, there were no atheists in our community, no agnostics or sceptics. I had never heard of an infidel. Everybody believed. Some were drunkards, others swore and cursed; many were given to lying and stealing. They did not even profess to be Christians, but they all believed. I did not know one who even questioned the authenticity of the Word of God.

Are there not millions in a similar situation? I have found them everywhere I have gone. In ancient Russia, let alone Spain, Italy and many other countries of Europe, as well as in America, there are literally millions who believe and yet who are not saved. And if millions who believe in Christ are not Christians then what does it mean to believe?

Finally one day I came across that little booklet that was used so often by Queen Mary in her personal work, *Safety, Certainty, and Enjoyment*, by Geo. Cutting, and as a result my doubts vanished. I was assured of my salvation, and from that day to this I have never had a doubt of any kind.

Three Steps

There are three steps in saving faith. They are like the three rungs of a ladder. The first two will not save, but the third will. However, you cannot take the third until you have taken the first two.

Hear

The first step I designate by the simple word "hear". "How shall they believe except they hear?" A knowledge of God's salvation is necessary before it is possible to believe. That is why we send missionaries to China, to India and to Africa. The heathen must first hear before they can believe. But I am sure that I need not dwell on this first step now. I am quite certain that everyone here present has again and again heard the message of God's salvation. Therefore you have already taken the first step. You have heard.

Believe

I designate the second step by using the simple word "believe". Now what is the meaning of "believe"? It simply means "giving intellectual assent to a truth". The Dictionary says, "to consent with the mind". When therefore you have given "intellectual assent to a truth" you have believed. You have taken the second step. But you are not saved.

When the King James translators were translating the Bible some three hundred and fifty years ago, they came across a certain Hebrew word in the Old Testament Scriptures, and they began searching for an English word with which to translate it. Finally they chose the word "trust", and that is why you have the word "trust" occurring so frequently in the Old Testament Scriptures. It is found a hundred and fifty-two times.

In due time they came to the New Testament, and presently they encountered the same word, but this time in the Greek, and again they searched for an English word with which to translate it. But for some unknown reason they decided to choose an entirely different word, for they chose the word "believe". Had they been consistent, had they used the Old Testament word for their translation, this message would not have been necessary. But they used, as I have stated, the word "believe", and that is why you have the word "believe" occurring so frequently in the New Testament Scriptures, especially in the Gospel of John and the epistles of Paul. That has caused all the confusion and misunderstanding.

You see, the word "believe" has to do with the head, the intellect. It is a mental process. But you can believe all you want to believe *about* Jesus Christ and still not be saved. You can believe everything that I believe about the Bible, and yet perish eternally. That is the faith of the demons. The Word of God declares that the demons also believe and tremble. They were among the first to acclaim Jesus as the Son of God, but they did not submit to Him. They believe as much or more than you do about Christ. They do not for a moment doubt His Deity, but their faith is purely intellectual. It does not change their lives, and their doom is certain, therefore they tremble.

I came across a certain denomination one day and I was anxious to discover, if I could, the basis upon which they received men and women as members of their churches. I learned that they asked them just one question, one question consisting of two parts, namely, "Do you believe God loves you and that Jesus Christ His Son died for you?" If they could answer that question in the affirmative they were accepted.

But who doesn't believe in the love of God? Everyone who believes the Bible does. And who doesn't believe that Jesus Christ died for mankind? The Bible says He did, and if you believe the Bible you believe He died for you. That doesn't make you a Christian. That doesn't change your life. That is purely intellectual. Thousands believe in the love of God and the death of Christ who are not Christians. The second step will save no one and yet that is where multitudes stop. They take the second step but not the third. Hence they are not yet saved.

What are the usual questions that are asked of one who wishes to join the church? These—"Do you believe in the virgin birth, the death, resurrection and second coming of Christ? Do you believe Christ died for your sins?" Such questions are doctrinal and can be answered intellectually by anyone. What are the questions I ask? These—"Have you been born again? Are you saved? Have you received Jesus Christ?" Such questions are experimental. If they can be answered in the affirmative I do not worry about the others.

TRUST

The third step and the only step that saves I designate by the simple word "trust". And now I must turn to *The New English Bible*. At long last the erroneous and misleading translation of the Authorized Version has been corrected. After 350 years the word "believe" has been eliminated. After preaching this sermon for 40 years I now have *The New English Bible* to back me.

When the Philippian jailer asked the question, "What must I do to be saved?" the answer in *The New English Bible* is, "Put your trust in the Lord Jesus, and you will be saved" (Acts 16: 30–31). Again and again instead of "believe" it is "Put your faith in" or "Put your trust in the Lord Jesus." That has nothing whatever to do with the intellect; that has to do with the will, and it demands a decision. Multitudes there are who "believe" who have never "trusted".

In the O.T. the way of salvation is stated thus—"Put your trust in the Lord" (Ps. 4: 5). In the N.T. it is, "Believe on the Lord." The O.T. has the correct translation. When you "put your trust in the Lord", you are saved.

Now what is the meaning of the word "trust"?

Excludes Effort

First, it excludes effort. Did you ever have anyone try to teach you to float? Do you remember how you stood beside your instructor in the water, and how he said to you, "The water can sustain your weight. All you have to do is to trust the water. Now throw yourself back and float." And do you remember how you threw yourself back on the water and how you floated—to the bottom?

Then do you recall how you stood again by your instructor and how he said to you, "Now why did you tighten your muscles? Why did you hold your breath? Couldn't you trust the water? Why, it carries whole navies. It can easily bear you up." And once again you threw yourself back on the water, but there was a slight catching of the breath, a tightening of the muscles and once again you floated—to the bottom.

Then again you stood beside your instructor. Again he urged you to trust, and this time without any effort of your own, as you threw yourself back on the water, to your pleasure and delight, you found yourself floating.

I wish someone would float tonight on God's great salvation. Put aside your effort. Stop struggling. Don't try to help yourself either by works or religion. Just float. Trust, I say, excludes effort. As long as you are putting forth effort you are not trusting.

Implies Committal

Second, trust implies committal. I think the best illustration is that of the marriage ceremony. Here is a young man who is keeping company with a young woman. For some considerable time they go together. At least they should. At last he asks the all-important question and she says, "Yes". Now they are engaged.

Now this young man makes a great many promises and the young woman believes he means what he says. After a while her girl friends come along and they ask her some questions. "We understand," they say, "that this young man of yours has promised you a home." "Yes, he has," replies the young woman. "And he has promised you clothes and food. Now tell us, do you have the home?" "Oh no," she exclaims, "I do not. I am still living with my parents." "What about the food?" they continue. "Does he supply your food?" "Why no, of course not," she responds, "except when we go to the restaurant, and then sometimes I pay the bill." "What about clothes? Has he given you any clothes?" "No, he has not," the young woman answers; "my parents still buy my clothes." "And yet you believe the young man," they exclaim. "Yes, I do," she answers. "I believe every word. I have no doubt of any kind." You see, she had taken the second step; she had believed.

There comes a never-to-be-forgotten day when the young man stands at the front of the church facing the minister, first on one foot, then on the other. Never in his life has he stood so long before. It seems an age. At last to the strains of the wedding march the young woman on the arm of her father comes slowly, oh, so slowly, down the aisle. Every eye is fastened on her. There is plenty of time for everyone to admire her wedding gown.

At last she reaches the front and stands beside the man of her choice. The minister asks one or two very important questions: "Wilt thou?" And she "wilts". Then something happens that has never happened before, and I want you to mark, if you will, very carefully, my phraseology. For the first time in her life she gives herself over, she hands herself to, she commits herself to, she trusts the young man. Taking his arm, she now leaves the church in his protection. Never again will she have to work. He is now responsible for her and it is up to him to look after her. Her worries are over. He must provide for her.

A little later her girl-friends approach her again. "Well," they ask, "has he given you a home?" "Oh yes," she exclaims, "we are now living together in our own home." "What about the food?" "Yes, he pays the grocery bills and the butcher bills. He provides the food." "And what about clothes?" "Yes, he is buying my clothes—not as many as I want, but all that I need. Indeed he is looking after everything."

But just when did she get everything? Was it when she took the second step, when she believed, or was it when she took the third step and trusted? It was not until she trusted. She had believed but she got nothing. When she trusted she got everything. So it is with salvation. You can believe as much as you want to believe and get nothing. But the very moment you give yourself up to Jesus Christ, the moment you hand yourself over to Him, the moment you commit yourself to Him, the moment you put your trust in Him, you are saved, but not until then.

Have you ever done it? You see, it implies committal. It is something you must do. Just as that young woman had to walk down the aisle and definitely give herself up to the young man of her choice for the rest of her life, so you must give yourself up to the Lord Jesus Christ for time and eternity, if you are to be saved. The second step will not save. The third is absolutely necessary. You must trust Jesus Christ. Will you then do what the young woman did? Will you too come down the aisle? Will you hand yourself over to the Heavenly Bridegroom as she did to the earthly? Will you own allegiance to Him? If you will, you will be His for evermore, and He will be responsible for you.

Here is a struggling swimmer who is drowning. He goes down for the first time struggling furiously, while a man stands on the bank with folded arms, who never makes a motion to dive in and rescue the drowning man. Now he is going down for the second time. Still he struggles. But still the man makes no effort to save him. Now he is going down for the third and last time. But he does not struggle. His arms fall limp at his sides, and in a feeble voice he cries out "Help!" And in a moment the man on the bank unfolds his arms, dives in and easily rescues the drowning man.

Why didn't he do it before? Because the man thought he could save himself. He had to wait until the man was ready to give up. But the moment the man was willing to trust his rescuer he was saved. As the rescuer approached him all he had to do was to commit himself to the one who had come to save him, and the moment he gave himself up to his rescuer and trusted him, that moment he was saved. When you, my friend, are willing to give yourself up to your Rescuer, the resurrected, living Christ, you too will be saved. What you believe about Him will not save you; you must put your trust in Him.

"Believe on the Lord Jesus Christ, and thou shalt be saved." Is that what I say when I am dealing with a lost soul? Of course not. If I were to say that I would have an argument on my hands at once. I would be asked the meaning of the word "believe". No, I do not use the King James Version. I use the Old Testament word, or The New English translation, and I say to the seeker: "Put your trust in the Lord Jesus, and you will be saved."

Requires Action

In the third place trust requires action. Let me show you what I mean.

It is a glorious morning. The mighty cataract of Niagara thunders on the rocks at the foot of the Falls. An eleven hundred foot tightrope has been stretched from bank to bank, on which Charles Blondin, the world's greatest tightrope walker, is to cross. Special trains from Toronto and Buffalo have been run to bring the crowds.

The date is June 30th, 1858.

Balancing his 40-pound pole he steps on the rope and starts across, while the voices of the throngs are hushed, until, as he triumphantly places his foot on the farther bank, a great cheer rises even above the noise of the cataract itself.

Turning to the sea of faces, he now makes a thrilling proposal. He offers to recross the cataract with a man on his back.

But who is to be the man? Excitedly the people talk among themselves.

"Do you believe I am able to carry you across?" at length asks the ropewalker, turning to a likely looking individual.

"I certainly do," at once responds the one addressed.

"Will you let me?" inquires the waiting hero.

"Will I let you? Well, hardly. You don't think I am going to risk my life like that, do you?" And he turns away.

"And what about you?" he asks Henry Colcord, his manager. "Do you believe I can carry you across?"

"I believe. In fact, I have no doubt about it at all," answers Colcord.

"Will you trust me?"

"I will!"

Breathlessly the people watch. The 38-foot pole is

balanced; they start; and the great rope tightens beneath their weight. Step after step, slow but sure, without hesitation, they move along. What confidence! The centre is reached. They are above the rushing, boiling, foam-covered water, the ugly rocks beneath, poised, as it were, in mid-air.

Now they are nearing the Canadian side. A great hush falls on the excited crowds. The people hold their breath. The strain is terrific. Suddenly there is a pause. Some gambler had cut the guy line and the rope is swaying fearfully. Blondin tells Colcord to dismount, which he does, standing with one foot on the rope and his hands on Blondin's shoulders.

"Harry," says Blondin, "you are no longer Colcord; you are now Blondin. Be part of me. If I sway, sway with me. Do not try to balance or we will both be dead."

Colcord climbs back. The rope sways wildly and Blondin begins running. How he keeps his balance no one knows, but he does, and at last they are over; the final step is taken, and they stand once more on terra-firma, while the spectators go wild with excitement. The tension is broken; the nerve-racking experience ended.

Bridging the gulf between time and eternity is the great rope of salvation. Never yet has it broken. And Jesus Christ alone is able to cross it. You may have heard all about it, and, like the first man, you may even believe that Jesus can carry you across. But not until you take the final step and commit yourself to Him will you ever get over. You may believe but you must also trust.

Oh my friend, tell me, have you trusted? Or do you merely believe in your head, and have you failed to take the last important step? If so, will you not by a definite act of your will "put your trust in the Lord Jesus?" If you will, "you will be saved." Will you do it? Do it and do it—NOW.

CHAPTER VI

THE WAY OF SALVATION

THERE are only two companies of people in this world today: those who are guilty and those who are not guilty, the saved and the lost, the sinners and the saints. And you, my friend, belong to onc or the other. You are either a Christian or you are not a Christian.

There are only two ways: the Broad Way that leads to destruction and death, and the Narrow Way that leads to Heaven and eternal life. And you, my fellow traveller, are on the one or the other, the Broad or the Narrow, for there is no third—no way between; you are either travelling to Heaven or to Hell.

There are only two Masters, God and the Devil, and you are serving either one or the other, for "no man can serve two masters". Therefore, let me ask you: To which company do you belong? Where are you going? Whom are you serving?

Over the one group is written the word "guilty", and over the other "not guilty", and "there is no difference". It matters not whether you have been very good or very bad, whcther you consider yourself a great sinner or a small sinner; you are guilty or not guilty.

You may have your name on the rolls of a thousand churches, you may be the most active worker in the church, or you may have spent the years of your life in the penitentiary for some great crime, but it makes no difference; if you are unsaved you are guilty—and you belong to the company that is travelling on the Broad Way to destruction.

You may be cultured and refined, and have many things to commend you, but God places you in the same class with the most debauched sinners of the world, and brands you "guilty". All in that company are not equally degraded, but all are equally guilty, "for there is no difference: for all have sinned and come short of the glory of God" (Rom. 3: 22–23).

The Great Deluge

What an awful picture presents itself as we think of the great deluge, when the flood destroyed the entire race with the exception of Noah and those who were with him in the ark! Sinners who had lived good moral lives, along with the most degraded and depraved, were drowned beneath the mighty waters that swept them into Eternity.

Only two classes, only two companies: those in the ark and those outside. It mattered not whether their sin had been small or great, whether their lives had been, as people say, good or bad; they had disobeyed God; they had refused to be warned and to enter the ark of safety, and there was no alternative. It was the ark or death.

Oh! the weeping and wailing as they clambered to the highest mountain peak, only to find that their prayers and tears came all too late, and availed them nothing; there was no escape. All alike must perish. They had neglected to enter the ark.

Not because you have committed murder, not because your hands are red with blood, will your doom be sealed, but because you have neglected the only Hope of escape offered you. Have you not ignored the unanswerable question: "How shall we escape, if we neglect so great salvation?" (Heb. 2: 3). Listen! "The wicked shall be turned into hell, and all the nations that forget God" (Ps. 9: 17). You may have lived a very good life outwardly, and may never once have committed any of the glaring, outstanding sins of the age, but you have neglected God's salvation, you have failed to enter the Ark of Safety, Jesus Christ, and therefore you are guilty, and must perish.

The Cities of the Plains

When God destroyed the cities of the plains, think you that all in Sodom and Gomorrah were equally sinful and degraded? Were there not sinners great and small? Was every man a criminal? By no means. But all were sinners, and therefore all were guilty before God. And when the fire and brimstone fell, it destroyed them all alike, old and young, great and small, good and bad. All were in the city and in the same company and all were branded "guilty".

The First-Born of Egypt

No one would think for a moment of saying that all the first-born of Egypt were equally depraved. Many were, no doubt, the finest living men of the land: statesmen, poets, philosophers and priests. But God said, "When I see the blood I will pass over you" (Exod. 12: 13). Therefore every house sprinkled by the blood was passed over, and every one not so sprinkled was smitten, and the eldest son slain. It was not a question of the heinousness of sin, it was a question of obedience. Was the blood there or not? And once again there were only two companies, those sheltered by the blood and those not so covered.

My brother, are you sheltered by the blood of Jesus Christ? Remember, "it is the blood that maketh an atonement for the soul" (Lev. 17: 11). "And without shedding of blood is no remission" (Heb. 9: 22). God has said in words that no man can alter: "When I see the blood I will pass over you" (Exod. 12: 13). Otherwise you must perish. Are you covered by the blood? If not, be warned:

the floods of God's judgment will overtake you. Death and eternity are still before you, and there is no escape.

All Guilty

In the great penitentiaries of the world you will find all classes, from murderers to conscientious objectors, sinners deep dyed, whose hands are red with blood, along with those who simply refused to take up arms and slay their fellow men, but thereby failed to obey the laws of their country—all guilty, and all under condemnation.

It is not necessary for a man to sink a mile below the surface of the water in order to drown. A foot will do quite as well. The horse that breaks the fence that encloses him in only one place gains his freedom just as completely as the one that breaks the entire enclosure.

So one sin will bar you out of Heaven, and place you in the company of the lost, just as surely as though you had transgressed a million times. For has God not said that "Whosoever shall keep the whole law, and yet offend in one point, he is guilty of all"? (Jas. 2: 10). Will you believe God's Word? Think of it, to fail in one point, to break only one commandment, to commit but one sin, and yet be guilty of all.

A Chain of Ten Links

Suppose I am hanging by a chain of ten links. Suddenly the chain breaks and I fall. Upon examination I find that only one link gave way; the other nine were still unbroken. And yet the chain broke. And so it is with sin. We are held by a law called the ten commandments; we break one, just one, and we are lost, for we have broken the law.

Have you kept the whole law? Has not one commandment been broken, and are you not guilty of at least one sin? I do not ask which it is, for that does not matter. It may be murder, or it may be falsehood; it may be adultery, or it may be theft. But if you have broken one commandment, if you have failed in one point, you have broken the law, and you are branded "guilty"; you are classed with the deepest-dyed sinners of the world. The wrath of the Almighty hangs over you, for you are under the condemnation of God.

The Greatest Sin

You tell me you are not guilty! You say you have never sinned! I want to tell you that you are guilty of the greatest sin it is possible for a human being to commit. I accuse you of the blackest crime of which man can be guilty. You have rejected the Lord Jesus Christ. You have spurned His love, ignored His pleadings and trampled underfoot His precious blood. You have refused to accept God's offer of mercy; and you are guilty of the sin of unbelief, the greatest sin that the Bible knows anything about. It is the sin of ingratitude.

God offers you the gift of His Son, and you, ungrateful wretch that you are, refuse His Gift. "When He (the Holy Spirit) is come," said Jesus, "He will reprove the world of sin." What kind? Murder? Adultery? Theft? No! Listen! "Of sin, because they believe not on me" (John 16: 8–9). Unbelief! That is the great unpardonable sin. You wouldn't dream of hurting the feelings of an earthly friend by refusing a gift, but you think nothing of rejecting God's Gift, upon whom depends your eternal salvation. And if you are not saved, then at this moment you are guilty of unbelief—the greatest sin it is possible to commit.

Not a Question of the Depth of Sin

It is not a question of the depth of sin. The question is: What is your attitude towards Jesus Christ? Have you owned Him as Saviour or not? There is no more important question than the one asked by Pilate: "What shall I do then with Jesus which is called Christ?" Your relation to Jesus Christ will determine your eternal destiny.

Will you plead "guilty" now? Are you not already convinced of sin? And do you not know that one sin will bar you out of Heaven eternally? You say it is not fair. But you forget that Heaven is a prepared place for a prepared people. It would not be just on God's part to allow you to enter Heaven with your sin, for you would be the most unhappy person there. How do you feel when you are thrown in the company of holy people? Do you enjoy it? Are you not more at home among your own associates in sin? You must be prepared, you must have a new nature and be born again to enjoy the things of God. Remember that nothing unholy can ever enter Heaven. Only the pure in heart will see God (Matt. 5: 8).

Wrong Conceptions of Salvation

Everywhere I go I find people who are living in a false experience and resting upon a false foundation, believing that they are saved when they are not. Thousands upon thousands of church-members, hundreds of professing Christians are unable to give a reason for their hope of Heaven. They think they are all right; they believe they are ready to meet God, and yet when asked a few simple questions their answers reveal the fact that they are as ignorant of God's way of salvation as the heathen in Africa.

The devil has blinded their eyes, stopped their ears, and darkened their understanding lest they should be undeceived and be converted. Their souls are shrouded in almost total night and it is Satan's business to keep them so. Many of them are active workers in the Church, faithful officials of its different boards and societies, good, moral and upright in their lives, but—unsaved.

It is because of this fact, because I know that souls are dying in the belief that all is well, that I want to make the way plain, and thus be the means of saving some from waking up in a lost Eternity. Oh, think of it! To be a professing Christian, a member of the church, and to pass out of this life fully expecting to enter Heaven, only to find the gate barred, and the door closed. How bitter, how awful the disappointment!

Oh, then, my friend, let me clear myself of your blood. Let me point out the way. And let me urge you, whether you are saved or not, to listen to what I say, lest you, even you, are deceived.

Man's Idea of Salvation

Inherent in the heart of man is the idea that he must do something in order to be saved. Far away in India there are men who, not knowing the grace of God, nor the fact that eternal life is a gift, attempt by works of merit and efforts of their own to achieve salvation. Here is one who lies on a bed of spikes in the scorching sun. Another swings over a low fire. Others take upon themselves vows of silence, or hold up a hand until it becomes fixed. Many crawl or walk hundreds of miles on pilgrimages, stretching their length on the ground every six feet. Thousands wash in the waters of the Ganges, thereby seeking to merit salvation.

So also with the Greek Orthodox Church, Judaism and Roman Catholicism—religions of works like all the rest. Doing, doing, doing! Oh, the awful bondage and slavery of man-made religion! How hard man makes it for himself. And all the while God has clearly and emphatically stated, again and again, that life is a gift and therefore can never be obtained by works. You must accept it as a gift or eternal life can never be yours.

"Work Out" Versus "Work For"

The Bible clearly says, "Work *out* your own salvation," but it nowhere says, "Work *for* your own salvation." You cannot even begin to work it out until God first of all works it in. And again, it does not say, "Work out your own atonement." Christ did that nineteen hundred years ago. What a hopeless task would be mine if I had to work out my own atonement! No one but the God-man could do that.

Here is a young man who enters college. He goes to the registrar, pays his fee, and is enrolled as a student.

"Now, young man," says the college registrar, "work out your college course." You see, he could not even begin to work until he had been enrolled as a student. And now through the next four or more years he will be working out his course of studies. You, also, my friend, must thus begin; you must get in before you can work at all. You work out what God works in, but you never, never work for God's gift.

Man Can Do Nothing

There is nothing that man can do to save himself. In the religions of the world, man-made blood flows from man to God. That is merit. But in Christianity it flows from God to man. That is grace. False shepherds, wolves in sheep's clothing, told our soldier boys that to die on the battlefield merited everlasting life, that if a man gave his life for his country he would go to Heaven. Thank God, the men themselves knew better, knew that they were not fit to meet a holy God.

Man, listen! All the blood of all men of all the battles of the world's history would not suffice to wash away even one sin; but the blood of the God-man, shed on Calvary's cross nineteen hundred years ago, once for all, is sufficient to wash away all the sins of all the men of all ages. Man can do nothing to merit eternal life. Long, long ago the Lord Jesus cried, "It is finished" (John 19: 30). What can man add to a finished work?

If morality, if man's righteousness is sufficient, then Christ need not have died. "For if righteousness come by the law, then Christ is dead in vain" (Gal. 2: 21). The greatest atrocity in the world's history was the death of Christ if man has power to save himself. God gave His Son because He knew that man was absolutely helpless, and needed a Saviour. Morality, my friend, will save no one, and morality will not save you.

The Pharisee and the Publican

"Two men went up into the temple to pray; the one a Pharisee, and the other a publican. The Pharisee stood and prayed thus with himself:

"God, I thank thee that I am not as other men are, extortioners, unjust, adulterers, or even as this publican. I fast twice in the week, I give tithes of all that I possess. And the publican, standing afar off, would not lift up so much as his eyes unto heaven, but smote upon his breast, saying, God be merciful to me a sinner" (Luke 18: 9–14).

With the Pharisee it was all "I". "I fast, I give, I am not, I do". That was religion and self-righteousness to the limit. And when you ask men today the ground of their salvation, they will answer by thousands, "I go to church, I give my tenth, I teach in Sunday-school, I have been baptised, I am an active church worker," and so on. It is all "I! I! I!" and there is no Christ in it at all. Not what "Christ" did, but what "I" do.

How different from Paul, the chief of sinners: "Not I, but Christ," he said. Let us take our place as sinners, for this is our eternal character, and boast of what Christ did, remembering that all our righteousness is but filthy rags; and that "Jesus paid it all".

Nothing either great or small,
Nothing sinner, no;
Jesus did it, did it all,
Long, long ago.

No Work Can Merit Salvation

You may be one of the most active members in the church, and still be unsaved, for church activity never saved anyone. Doctrine and dogma, prayers, self-denial, tithes, tears and penitence, though good enough in their place, will not save you. No man, minister or priest can do that. "Neither is there salvation in any other; for there is none other name under heaven given among men, whereby we must be saved" (Acts 4: 12). Christ, and Christ alone, can save.

There is no work, either moral or religious, that can merit in any degree whatever God's salvation. The best life that man can live, along with the most active church work he can do, does not bring him one step nearer God. Beautiful as morality is, precious as works of righteousness, mercy, philanthropy, and sacrificial service on behalf of others may be, they cannot merit salvation, nor gain favour with God. Let us start right, for salvation is "not of works, lest any man should boast (Eph. 2: 9). So then, my friend, if you are depending upon what you are and what you are doing, you are lost. Self can never save.

The Divine Plan of Salvation

Man's plan of salvation is always based on merit. God's on grace. God says: "By grace are ye saved" (Eph. 2: 8). And grace is the very opposite of merit; the one excludes the other. If salvation is by grace, it cannot be through merit; and if it is through merit, it cannot be by grace. It is wholly of merit or wholly of grace.

Grace is one of the greatest words in the Bible. "The Gospel of the grace of God" is the good news that we are given to proclaim. One of the most wonderful statements ever made about God's salvation is found in Romans 3: 24, where it says: "Being justified freely by His grace through the redemption that is in Christ Jesus." Every word is pregnant with meaning.

Take, for instance, that grand word "redemption", which means "to buy back". The race had been sold to Satan, sin and death, by the first Adam. Jesus Christ came and paid the ransom by taking upon Himself sin and its penalty, and so wrought redemption. He bought us back from the slave-market of Satan.

Thus He paid the sinner's ransom,
Bore the awful penalty;
Bled and died to make atonement,
Blessed Lamb of Calvary!

And the price He paid was His own life's blood. "Ye were not redeemed," declares the inspired apostle, "with corruptible things, as silver and gold; but with the precious blood of Christ" (1 Pet. 1: 18–19). Hence, now that the ransom price has been fully paid, God is able to justify "freely".

In John 15: 25, you have the same Greek word which is here translated "freely", rendered, "without a cause". "They hated me without a cause." That is, without any reason or ground for their hatred. And that is the way that God justifies the sinner. It is "without a cause", "freely". There is nothing good in us that merits His favour. He justifies wholly on the ground of the redemptive work of Jesus Christ.

Thus grace is "unmerited favour"; and salvation is of grace, freely bestowed upon the undeserving; it is all of

God. Man can do nothing to merit or deserve it. It can neither be earned nor purchased.

There are two ways to satisfy the law. One is to keep it; the other is to bear its penalty if broken. Its penalty was "death". "The wages of sin is death" (Rom. 6: 23). "The soul that sinneth, it shall die" (Ezek. 19: 4). Law always carries with it a penalty and the law cannot be broken without incurring the penalty.

But God, desiring to save the sinner, and yet deal in justice, "that He might be just and the justifier of him which believeth in Jesus" (Rom. 3: 26), gave Christ "to be the propitiation" or "satisfaction" for man's sin—"Whom God hath set forth to be a propitiation through faith in His blood, to declare His righteousness" (Rom. 3: 25). "And He (Jesus) is the propitiation for our sins; and not for ours only, but also for the sins of the whole world" (1 John 2: 2). Thus He made it possible by bearing the penalty of sin, which was death, for God to deal with man in grace.

The Prevalent Idea of Repentance

How hard it is to get men to just simply take God at His Word and believe what He says! They will insist on "doing" something in order to gain His favour. Take for instance the prevalent idea regarding repentance. Inherent in the very nature of man is the idea that God demands a long period of contrition and sorrow, bitter remorse and anguish of heart, hours of prostration at the "penitent form" where he confesses his sins and prays for forgiveness and salvation, before he can obtain mercy. And this he calls "repenting of his sins".

Well, convicted he may be; but conviction is not repentance, nor does it constitute conversion. And it is clear from God's Word that such an experience is by no means the basis of salvation. Nowhere does God tell an unsaved man to go through a period of so-called repentance (which is not repentance) in the hope that if he thus "repents of his sins" long enough, God will on that ground pardon him at last.

It is not thy tears of repentance and prayers,
But the Blood that atones for thy soul.

Suppose you do repent of your sins, pray for forgiveness and salvation, confess your transgressions to God, and plead for mercy and pardon unceasingly—will that save you? Can you merit God's favour by such works? You know you cannot.

There must come a moment in the midst of it all when you turn from everything of your own "doing"—tears, prayers, confession and repentance, and trust Christ alone, receive Him, rely on His shed blood, place your faith in the finished work of Calvary, believing that "Jesus paid it all".

Places God in a Wrong Light

Such an attitude places God in an altogether wrong light. We were giving out tracts one day, urging upon all we met to take them. Now, suppose a man should come crawling behind us on his hands and knees, begging for a tract, what would people think of us? They would say something like this: "Look at those mean men. That poor fellow is begging for a tract and they simply turn their backs on him and go on." But no, that was not our attitude at all. It was the joy of our hearts to give them away. All he needed to do was to get up and take one.

Don't you see it? God's back is not toward mankind. Men do not need to plead and beg and coax Him to save them. Why, that is what He is waiting to do. That was the reason for which He gave His Son. He stands with His face towards a fallen race, bending down in love and mercy, crying, "Come, take, trust, receive!" And when man prays and entreats where he ought to be accepting and praising, it puts God in an attitude of one who is unwilling and must be entreated, whereas it is man, ungrateful man, who is unwilling.

God is offering a gift, the gift of eternal life, and beseeching men to accept it. Do men beg for the Christmas present as it is held out to them? Not if they know the giver. They would not insult his sincerity by pleading for that which had already been offered. They would simply take it and say, "Thank you". Then let us change our minds about God's attitude, accept His gift, and thank Him.

I take the life of Jesus Christ,
'Tis all that I can do;
The Holy Spirit re-creates,
And I am born anew.

Yes, it is as simple as that. You take by faith and the Holy Spirit does the rest. The atoning death of Christ is the basis or ground of salvation, and faith is the connecting link between the sinner and Christ. Faith is relying upon God's provision. Oh then, "Put your trust in the Lord Jesus, and you will be saved" (Acts 16: 31, N.E.B.). Will you do it? Do it and do it—NOW.

CHAPTER VII

THE FALSE AND THE TRUE

THERE are a great many things that people are doing in order to get to Heaven. False foundations abound on every side. In what do we hope? Why do we expect God to let us enter Heaven? Upon what ground are we standing? These are the questions that must be answered, and they are of paramount importance. First then the False and after that the True.

THE FALSE

1. *The Christian Religion*

The first false foundation that I want to mention is the Christian Religion. What is religion? It is something that man does. When we speak of a "religious man", we mean one who has been baptised, goes to church, partakes of the Lord's supper, gives his tenth, and so on. Such a one is spoken of as a "good churchman", a "religious man".

Now the word "religion" is only used five times in the New Testament, four times in a bad sense and once in a reference to the believer's good works, but never as synonymous with salvation or spirituality. The so-called "Christian Religion", apart from Christ, has no more power to save than has Buddhism or Mohammedanism. Yet it is in this system, the "Christian Religion", that millions—Catholics, Coptic, Greek Orthodox and Protestant—are trusting for salvation.

Do you know that it is possible to be converted without being regenerated? I verily believe that tens of thousands who have been converted will never get to Heaven, because they have not been born again. They have been converted from certain forms of sin, converted from scepticism and indifference, and in many cases converted to some denomination, but not to God; converted to the church and to respectability, but not born again, not regenerated. And, remember, "Except a man be born again, he cannot see the Kingdom of God" (John 3: 3).

Pundita Ramabai, the noted Indian Christian leader, was such a one. She herself tells the amazing story. Converted from Hinduism and other false systems of religion to Christianity, she accepted baptism and joined the church, and for eight years she lived a most consistent life.

But Pundita Ramabai was not a Christian. She herself says that she had never experienced the new birth. Christ as her personal Saviour she did not know. She had accepted Christianity, but not the Christ of Christianity.

But there came an hour in her life when, for the first time, she saw herself as a lost sinner needing a Saviour, and then came the great change. From that hour all life was different. She then knew the Christ of Christianity. She was born again; not merely converted, but regenerated by the Holy Spirit. Here is her testimony in her own words:

"I thought that repentance of sin and the determination to give it up was what was necessary for forgiveness; that the rite of baptism was the means of regeneration; and that my sins were truly washed away when I was baptised in the name of Christ. These and other such ideas, which are akin to Hindu mode of religious thought, stuck to me. I came to know, after eight years from the time of my baptism, that I had found the Christian religion, but had not found Christ, who is the Life of the religion. I needed Christ and not merely His religion."

Friend, what about you? Have you, too, been converted, but not regenerated? Do you know the Christ of Christianity as your personal Saviour? If not, I warn you that you will never enter Heaven. "Ye must be born again."

2. *Church Membership*

Now the next false foundation is church membership. Do you know that you can't join the Church? Let me explain. Suppose you were to join the royal family, do you think that that would cause the blood of the king of England to flow through your veins? Of course not! There is only one way by which such a thing could be accomplished. You would have to be born into the family. And so it is with the Church. I am not thinking now of the Catholic and Protestant churches; no, nor of any special denomination, but rather of the Church the only true Church, the great invisible Church of God, the Body of Christ.

God sets forth the Church as a great family, the family of God, and no one can join that family; he must be born into it. He can no more have the life of God throbbing in his heart by simply joining a church, than he can have royal blood flowing through his veins without being born into the family.

My friend, have you ever been born into the family of God? Are you a member of the true Church? Have you been born again? Or have you merely allowed your name to be placed on the roll of some local church? Church membership can never save. There is no church in the world that has power to save. Christ alone can do that. Hence, "Except a man be born again, he cannot see the kingdom of God." (John 3: 3).

There will be no Presbyterians in Heaven, remember; no Methodists or Baptists. Nor will there be any Plymouth Brethren, Anglicans, Evangelical Christians, Lutherans, Disciples, Roman or Greek Catholics. All man-given labels will be left outside, and only the blood-washed, those who possess eternal life, will be admitted. The question is not, "Am I a member of a church?" It is this: "Do I belong to the Lord Jesus Christ? Is my name written in the Lamb's Book of Life? Am I a sinner saved by grace?"

3. *Asceticism*

Another false foundation is asceticism. Men, realising something of the burden of sin, decide to enter upon a life of constant self-denial and meritorious deeds in an effort to save themselves, thus becoming ascetics.

The theory is that it is impossible to be saved in this world on acount of the many temptations to which humanity is subject. Hence, withdrawing from the world, the seeker lives apart in a cave or a monastery, and endures all kinds of physical privations in order to earn salvation. Many go on long pilgrimages to so-called holy places.

Thus acted "Uncle Vlas", a well-known character, depicted in a poem by the famous Russian poet, Nekrasoff, formerly a notorious sinner, as well as many others in Russia in days gone by. Night and day they repented, wept bitterly, and in divers ways tormented themselves—renouncing the world, fasting and praying continuously. Yet in spite of all their efforts, they remained unsatisfied, still afraid of death and, in many cases, longing to return to the world. Self-salvation they found to be an impossibility.

The Bible clearly and emphatically states that Christ died for our sins and provided a full and perfect salvation. Our own works, it declares, cannot save us. "Wherefore", writes Paul to those who sought by their own works to perfect themselves, "why are ye subject to ordinances (touch not; taste not; handle not;) after the commandments and doctrines of men?" (Col. 2: 20–23).

4. *Baptism*

Still another false foundation is Baptism. Now I believe in water baptism with all my heart, but I do not believe that baptism is necessary for salvation.

If such is your position, then you have forgotten that Paul said, "Christ sent me not to baptise, but to preach the gospel" (1 Cor. 1: 17). And think you that Paul would have gone away and left his work half done if baptism were necessary for salvation? Suppose the convert died before someone came along to baptise him, what then?

Remember, the thief on the cross was not baptised. And if there is one exception, that is sufficient.

Dare anyone say that none of the Friends, or Quakers, or members of the Salvation Army are saved, that there will be none of them in Heaven? They neither baptise nor partake of the Lord's Supper. Be careful now! If baptism is essential to salvation, they are going, every last one of them, to Hell.

"But," you explain, "the answer in the Catechism to the question, 'Who gave you this name?' is, 'My Sponsors in Baptism; wherein I was made a member of Christ, the child of God, and an inheritor of the kingdom of heaven.'" True, but do you know that you are quoting from fallible man and not from God's Word? It is utterly false. You may have been baptised and confirmed and still be a child of the devil, for rites and ceremonies have nothing whatever to do with salvation.

"He that believeth and is baptised shall be saved, but he that believed not shall be damned" (Mark 16: 16). To believe the Gospel is the important thing. Apart from believing, baptism has no meaning. Note carefully that Jesus did not say, "he that is not baptised shall be damned," but, "he that believeth not". Faith is absolutely essential to salvation; but nowhere do the Scriptures state that baptism is essential (1 Cor. 1: 17; Acts 20: 21).

Baptism never precedes faith. If it does, then it becomes unbeliever's baptism.

"Except a man be born of water and of the Spirit" (John 3: 5). Water here, as elsewhere, when used of spiritual birth, means "the Word of God" (Eph. 5: 26; 1 Pet. 1: 23).

There is one incident in God's Word that settles for ever the question of baptism in relation to salvation, namely, the conversion of Cornelius and his household (Acts 10: 43–8, 11: 14–17). The Holy Spirit fell on them, they spoke in tongues, they believed, they were granted repentance unto life, and they were saved, so these verses tell us. And yet it was after all this that they were baptised.

Suppose you go on in your sin after you have been baptized, are you still saved? Does not salvation deliver you, change you, and make you a new creature? "Thou shalt call His name Jesus: for He shall save His people from their sins" (Matt. 1: 21). Not in their sins, mark you, but from their sins. And if you are not saved from your sins you are not saved at all. Can baptism do that?

Last of all—and this is an unanswerable argument—to make baptism a condition of salvation contradicts the whole of the great Pauline teaching regarding the grace of God. Over and over again, we are told throughout the New Testament that faith is the only condition of salvation—and this mass of unmistakable evidence cannot be brushed aside. Thousands have experienced the new birth when pointed to such texts as the following alone: John 1: 12; 3: 14–18, 36; 5: 24; 6: 47; Acts 10: 43; 13: 39; 16: 31; Rom. 1: 16; 3: 19–26; 4: 5; Gal. 2: 16; Eph. 2: 8–9; Phil. 3: 9. What are we to say, then, when God's Spirit bears witness with our spirit that we are born of God, even though we have not been baptised?

Salvation is either of works or of grace, but not both. Paul has made that very clear in Romans and Galatians, especially. He wrote to prove conclusively that salvation was all of grace, and "not of works, lest any man should boast" (Eph. 2: 9). Then, whatever man may do, whether it be keeping the law, being baptised and confirmed, partaking of the Lord's Supper, or anything else, it is works! Oh, this doing, doing, doing! Man, Christ did it on Calvary! Stop doing and believe.

5. *Mediation*

Then there is the false foundation of Mediation. By mediation, I refer to the worship of the virgin Mary and the Saints, in whose mediation with Jesus Christ many are trusting. The point of view held is as follows: "I am a great sinner and therefore cannot possibly save myself, but I have mediators in Heaven whose merits and intercession on my behalf can open the doors of the Kingdom to me. They will pray for me and their prayers will influence Christ." Thus many sinners, who do not want to part with their sins, depend upon somebody's influence with God.

Neither the virgin Mary nor the saints can do anything for sinful man. Salvation was not accomplished either by the virgin Mary or the saints, but by Christ, and through Him alone we have access to God, for "there is none other name under heaven given among men, whereby we must be saved" (Acts 4: 12). "There is one Mediator between God and men, the man Christ Jesus" (1 Tim. 2: 5). One, mark you, and not even two, and that One not the virgin Mary nor a saint, but the Lord Jesus Christ Himself.

If a well-known advocate undertakes to plead your cause, why should you turn to others of inferior qualifications? Our heavenly Advocate, our only Mediator, as the Scriptures plainly state, is the Lord Jesus Christ. If He is sufficient, and God says He is, then why turn to others?

My friend, you need not be afraid to go to Him with your sin. He receives everyone. He is the Friend of sinners. But if you insist on going to others, unwilling to part with your sins, it will avail you nothing, for no one else can help you in the least.

6. *Keeping The Commandments*

One of the most popular of the false foundations is that of keeping the Commandments. Is this *your* hope? Well, suppose you should succeed in keeping them all, you would only have a negative experience. Salvation does not consist of a number of "don'ts". It is not "do" or "don't" but "done". Not what you "do" but what Christ "did". It is His work, not yours, that counts.

Here is a man who has but a few minutes to live. "What must I do to be saved?" he cries. "Keep the commandments," you reply. "Keep the commandments!" exclaims the dying man. "But I haven't time to begin. I am dying." Ah yes, true, too true! No time to even start keeping commandments on a death-bed. If keeping the law is man's only hope of salvation, then he is doomed already, for Jesus plainly and emphatically says, "None of you keepeth the law" (John 7: 19). And if you think you do, read thoughtfully Matthew 5: 27, 28, and 22: 34–40. Then read the tenth commandment.

But suppose you do keep the commandments, that will not impart life—eternal life. I don't take God's name in vain. I don't murder, steal, or commit adultery. I may keep all the commandments, including the observance of the Jewish sabbath, and yet ignore Jesus Christ and His atoning death. God does not promise eternal life simply because I don't do certain things. Ah, no, my friend, keeping the commandments will never impart life. Listen: "If there had been a law given which could have given life, verily righteousness should have been by the law" (Gal 3: 21).

7. *Prayers For The Dead*

Another false foundation is Prayers for the Dead. "If in this life I do not get saved, there is still hope for me.

I may obtain salvation after I am dead." Such is the belief of many a professing Christian in the established churches of the day. How do they expect to be saved after death? "Oh," they say, "the church will pray for the repose of our souls."

Such a basis of salvation is against all common sense and also against all justice, for relying upon it the sinner indulges freely in iniquity, believing that after death the church will pray him through. When the rich man in Hades longed for alleviation from his torment, he was told that between him and Lazarus there was a great gulf and that it was fixed so that neither he nor Lazarus could cross it. Hence escape was impossible (Luke 16: 26). No church could pray him out.

God accepts every sinner who sincerely repents, and justifies him on the basis of faith alone in the shed blood of the Lord Jesus Christ, thus bestowing upon him the gift of eternal life. Instead, therefore, of continuing in sin in this world with the hope that someone after death will pray for you and thus get you out of purgatory, the thing to do is to repent now and accept Jesus Christ as your Saviour while you are still here. "Behold, now is the accepted time; behold, now is the day of salvation" (2 Cor. 6: 2).

8. *Doing The Best I Can*

Perhaps your false foundation is doing the best you can. But let me ask you this question: "Was there ever a time when you failed just once to do the best you could?" You admit that there have been times when you could have done better than you did. Then on your own confession you are lost, for if "doing the best you can" is the ground upon which you base your salvation, you must perish, because you know perfectly well that no one has ever lived up to all the light he has and done his best at every point. The ground, therefore, upon which you stand has given way.

9. *Reformation*

Finally, there is the false foundation of Reformation. Men talk of "turning over a new leaf", which is absolute folly. The schoolboy makes a blot of ink on his copy-book and at once turns over a fresh page, clean and white. His teacher comes along to see his work and the new leaf looks splendid. But she wants to see what has been done already; and turning back the page, lo, and behold! the awful blot of ink. It is all very well, my friend, to turn over a new leaf, but what about the old ones?

"What about your record?" exclaims someone. "Have you no blots of sin on your life, and are you not afraid to have God turn back the pages? Ah, yes, I have, for "all have sinned". And yet I am not afraid. "Why?" you ask. Well, let me tell you about Martin Luther.

The devil, so the story goes, at one time came to Luther with a great scroll in his hands, written on both sides.

"What is this?" asked Luther.

"This," replied Satan, "is the record of your sins."

Very closely Luther examined the document, and found the devil's answer to be true, only too true. In fact, sins he had long since forgotten were there recorded, and he had to admit that he was guilty.

"Well," responded Luther, at length, "and is this all?"

"Oh no," exclaimed his Satanic Majesty, "by no means. There is yet another."

"Go," said Luther, "bring it to me."

In a few moments the devil returned with a second scroll similar to the first. And again the great reformer had to plead guilty.

"Is this all?" inquired Luther.

"No, there is one more," said Satan.

"Go, then; bring it too," commanded Luther.

Soon the devil returned with a third scroll which Luther closely scanned.

"Yes," admitted he, "these are all my sins. I committed them, every one. Are there still others?"

"No," answered Satan, "these are all."

Quietly Luther reached over to his desk, and, taking up a pen, he dipped it in a bottle of red ink, and then, taking the scrolls one by one, he wrote triumphantly across each one these words: "The blood of Jesus Christ His Son cleanseth us from all sin" (1 John 1: 7).

With a look of disappointment and rage on his face, the devil turned and disappeared.

So, my friend, I too, have sinned, and I, like Luther, am guilty. But, thank God, years ago I accepted Jesus Christ as my Saviour, and He washed my sins away. And now, I, too, can write across the pages of my poor, unworthy life, those magic words. My sins are blotted out, and, praise God, they will never again be remembered against me. God sees me in His Son, clothed in the faultless righteousness of Jesus Christ, and my sins all under the blood.

Reformation is not regeneration. You may paint up the old village pump, and make it the most beautiful in all the countryside, but if the water is bad, no amount of improvement on the outside will ever make it pure. Ah, no, the trouble is within, and it is still nothing but an old, painted hypocrite. You will have to take off the planks and go down, down to the very bottom of the well and find the poison that has defiled the water. It must be cleaned out. And so away down deep in the heart of man is a cesspool of sin, which no amount of outward improvement or refinement will ever effect in the least. The trouble is with the heart.

Law and education may deal with certain forms in which sin exhibits itself, such as intemperance, thieving, murder and the like, and thus, these specific forms of evil be made impossible, and the world, like the old painted pump, appear to be improving, but for sin itself there is absolutely nothing but the blood of Jesus, no other remedy. It is the inside of the cup and platter that must be cleansed. Let us go to the heart of the disease and apply the blood remedy.

Nothing can for sin atone,
Nothing but the blood of Jesus!
Naught of good that I have done,
Nothing but the blood of Jesus!

No surgeon, when dealing with an abscess, is going to plaster it over so that it looks better. If he knows his business, he knows that the knife must go in and that the abscess must be opened or cut out before healing is possible. And woe betide the man who ignores the sin-cancer, and seeks by reformation and outward improvement to effect a cure!

John Bunyan

One of the most striking examples of reformation is the experience of John Bunyan. Here is his confession in his own words:

"I betook me to my Bible, and began to take great pleasure in reading. Wherefore I fell to some outward reformation both in my words and life, and did set the commandments before me for my way to Heaven; then I thought I pleased God as well as any man in England.

"Thus I continued about a year; all of which time our neighbours did take me to be a very godly man, a new and religious man, and did marvel much to see such a great and famous alteration in my life and manners; and, indeed, so it was, though yet I knew not Christ, nor grace, nor faith, nor hope; for, as I have well seen since, had I then died, my state had been most fearful.

"But I say, my neighbours were amazed at this, my great conversion, from prodigious profaneness to something like a moral life. Now, therefore, they began to praise, to commend, and to speak well of me, both to my face and behind my back. Now I had, as they said, become godly.

"But oh! when I understood those were their words and opinions of me, it pleased me mighty well, for, though as yet I was nothing but a poor painted hypocrite, yet I loved to be talked of as one that was truly godly. I was proud of my godliness, and, indeed, I did all that I did, either to be seen of, or to be well spoken of, by men."

So John Bunyan's reformation did not save him. Nor will your reformation, my friend, save you.

These, then, are some of the false foundations. Is yours one of them? Are you standing on sinking sand or are you trusting Jesus Christ, the Rock of Ages, for the salvation of your soul? Let no one deceive you. Salvation is through Christ and Christ alone. All else is vain. Man's way cannot avail.

The True

Having dealt with The False, now let us turn to The True.

On a memorable afternoon in Palestine, four thousand years ago, two weary travellers might have been seen, slowly toiling up the side of Mount Moriah—father and son, Abraham and Isaac.

"Behold the fire and the wood: but where is the lamb for a burnt offering?" inquires the son.

"My son," answers the Spirit-inspired father, "God will provide Himself a lamb for a burnt offering."

And now the altar has been erected and Isaac is laid upon it. Abraham grasps the knife and, with arm uplifted, prepares to plunge it into the heart of his son, when, suddenly, a voice from above cries out:

"Abraham, Abraham . . . lay not thine hand upon the lad. . . . And Abraham lifted up his eyes, and looked, and behold behind him a ram caught in a thicket by his horns; and Abraham went and took the ram, and offered him up for a burnt offering in the stead of his son."

"In the stead of his son." And hundreds of years after, God Himself provided a Lamb, His own well-beloved Son, to die "in the stead of" sinful, guilty man. But when He hung on the cross there was no voice from Heaven, for there was no other who could take His place. And so He died. Jesus Christ, a Substitute for you and for me.

Christ, the Son of God,
Bore the sinner's rod;
Hung upon the tree,
Died instead of me.

This, then, is the ground of Salvation. Christ's work is the only true foundation, and every other is sinking sand. Hence, salvation is "not of works". Christ did the work on Calvary's cross nineteen hundred years ago.

1. *The Nature of His Work*

If Calvary teaches anything at all, it teaches substitution. Such is the plain and unmistakable interpretation of Abraham's sacrifice of the ram, which, we are told, he offered up "in the stead of" Isaac his son. That was what the Holy Spirit meant when He wrote through the prophet: "The Lord hath laid on Him the iniquity of us all" (Isa. 53: 6). God took your sin and mine and laid it on His Son, Jesus Christ, who bore it, and died in our stead.

It is the great day of Atonement. The high priest leads a goat into the centre of the vast assembly. Laying his hands on the head of the goat, he confesses the sins of the people over it. Then it is led by a man away into the wilderness. Just as the scapegoat bore the sins of the Israelites, so the Lamb of God became our sin-bearer, and bore our guilt. Hence, it was written of Him:

"Behold the Lamb of God, which taketh away the sin of the world" (John 1: 29).

In that awful hour when darkness covered Golgotha, and at the moment when the Lord Jesus Christ sent out that piercing, never-to-be-forgotten cry: "My God, my God, why hast thou forsaken me!"—then it was that the foul thing called Sin, yours and mine, was laid upon Him. So terrible was the experience, that even God Himself had to turn away His face—Jesus was compelled to bear it alone.

He saw my fallen state,
And knew my awful fate;
He bore the penalty
That I must bear, or He.

2. *The Sufficiency of His Work*

"It is finished!" was the cry that echoed over Golgotha as He neared the end of His gigantic task (John 19: 30). Oh what a glorious, triumphant cry it was! The work of man's redemption finished, completely accomplished at last. Nothing more to be done. Salvation provided.

Isn't the Father fully satisfied? Ah, yes! Jesus has met every demand of the law. "He hath made Him to be sin for us, who knew no sin; that we might be made the righteousness of God in Him" (2 Cor. 5: 21). Does man honour God by attempting to add to a finished work? He can do nothing but accept and rest upon what has already been done.

Nothing either great or small,
Nothing sinner, no—
Jesus did it, did it all,
Long, long ago.

3. *The Motive of His Work*

But what was it that caused Him to make such a sacrifice? What could it be but love? "God commendeth his love toward us, in that, while we were yet sinners, Christ died for us" (Rom. 5: 8). Was love the cause of the atonement or was the atonement the cause of love? It was love that caused the atonement. God's great heart of infinite love and compassion felt so deeply for man in his lost estate that He, of His own free will, gave Jesus Christ, His only begotten Son, to die. Oh, what wondrous love! Who can fathom its depths! To think that God, the great, omnipotent God, "so loved that He gave"!

God loves the sinner but hates his sin. It isn't that He loves us when we're good and hates us when we're bad, as some parents teach their children. He loves us just the same as He always has all the time, but He loathes the sin that separates us from Him, just as a father loves his child when it has smallpox and at the same time hates the disease that isolates the child from him.

You did not ask God to love you. It was freely bestowed. He took the initiative. Oh, my brother, my sister, think of it!—God loves you! It matters not who you are nor what you have done—God loves you! You may be the most debauched sinner in the world, the most miserable wretch that ever breathed, I care not—God loves you! How can you spurn such love, such matchless love?

4. *The Scope of His Work*

The scope of His work is universal. "Him that cometh to me I will in no wise cast out," He declared (John 6: 37). "Whosoever" is the word He uses over and over again to denote the universality of His work. And that big word, "whosoever" just means you. Put your own name wherever you find it. Make it personal. You have the right to say,

'Twas for me He suffered so,
Drank the bitter cup of woe,
For I nailed Him to the tree,
And He died, He died for me.

Ah, yes, the vilest of the vile as well as the best; sinners of the deepest dye as well as the good and moral. None have gone too far, none have sunk too low. The Lord Jesus is able to save the worst that can be found. You are not too great a sinner. He can save even you.

In fact, the sinner is the only one who has any claim on Him at all. "Christ Jesus came into the world to save sinners" (1 Tim. 1: 15). And Jesus Himself said: "I came not to call the righteous, but sinners to repentance" (Mark 2: 17). If you insist that you are good enough already, then you have no need of Him at all. But if you are a poor, guilty, lost and undone sinner, having no righteousness of your own, you are the very one for whom He came.

Oh, my friend, let me beseech you in the name of my Saviour, to take your place now, this moment, as a lost and guilty sinner, and claim the sinner's Saviour. Rely on His work for you, not on yours for Him. Admit that you have nothing to offer, that you have no merit of your own, and rest upon what He did for you on Calvary's cross. Plant your feet firmly on the Rock, Christ Jesus, for it is His righteousness, His work, that must be the ground of your salvation.

I have now pointed out both The False and The True. "I call heaven and earth to record this day against you, that I have set before you life and death; therefore choose life." Choose, God says. A decision must be made, and you must make it. Therefore, choose and choose Christ. "Put your trust in the Lord Jesus, and you will be saved." Will you do it? Do it and do it—NOW.

CHAPTER VIII

THE GREATEST GIFT EVER OFFERED

WE ARE standing at the gate of Nain. A casket is being borne through the streets with the corpse of a young man, the only son of his mother, and she a widow.

Suddenly the mourners are interrupted by a man who hurries forward, gesticulating wildly.

"Here, let me deal with the dead," he cries. "I can bring him back to life."

Instantly the procession halts, and the bearers, with a mystified expression on their faces, gaze at the speaker as he elbows his way through the crowd.

"All this man needs is education," explains the interrupter, boldly approaching the casket in which lay the body of the departed. And out of his books of science and philsophy he attempts to instruct the young man lying in the casket at his feet.

But in vain he watches for a sign of returning life; there is no response. *Education* has failed. He forgets that birth and life precede education, that a man must be alive before he can be educated.

Presently another approaches, declaring that he has the secret of life.

"All that this man requires," he proclaims, "is a better environment. How can you expect to influence him under such unsanitary conditions?" And he points to the refuse and dirt on the ground.

So he goes to work. The rubbish is cleared away and

beautiful flowers artistically arranged around the casket. But in vain he looks for the returning flush of life; the man is still a corpse. And *Social Service* has also failed.

Suddenly a third man appears, and, pushing the other two aside, insists that he can succeed.

"Now, young man," he begins, "make up your mind that you are going to live. Exert your willpower. Brace yourself. You can get up if only you will." And thus he appeals to him.

"Come, young man," he continues, now playing on his affections, "reform, reform! See your poor, sorrowing, widowed mother. For her sake come back to life."

But there is no response, and at last he grows desperate.

"Here, sign this pledge," he exclaims, holding a small card before him. "I promise, God helping me, that I will never die again."

But—he is dead, dead, dead! And *Reformation* has failed.

Then there comes a pause. For a few moments no one moves. At last, however, a famous rabbi walks slowly towards the bier.

"My friends," he cries, "do you not know what this man needs? Religion! Through a knowledge of the five books of Moses and the Talmud he will be revived." And he sits down by the side of the bier."

"Now," declares the rabbi, "I will reveal to the young man the 613 precepts of the Law, for if he will keep them faithfully he will live again."

"But," inquires one of the bystanders, "how can a corpse observe them since he cannot even hear your words?"

"Ah, my son," exclaims the surprised rabbi, "I did not think of that." And sadly he turns away, for *Religion* also has failed.

Then from out of the crowd there steps the Figure of One who moves with perfect confidence and composure toward the scene of failure. A sudden hush falls on the expectant throng as He stands for a moment beside the bier.

Will this One also fail? Does He know the secrets of life and death?

Presently he speaks. His voice is calm but authoritative. "Young man, I say unto thee, arise!"

Eagerly the people crowd around to see. Who is this? "I say!" "I." What power is there behind that "I"? What manner of Man is this?

Suddenly their questions are answered. The eyelids quiver, the flush returns to the cheek; the heart throbs once more, and the young man rises to his feet.

What had happened? *Jesus* had imparted life. The man was dead, and it was *Life* he needed first and foremost, physical life. The Son of God knew that and gave it.

So it is with you, my friend, for you too are dead, "dead in trespasses and sins". And you too need life. But the life that you need is not physical, but spiritual. And it too is in Christ, and it is the Greatest Gift Ever Offered.

The Living Dead

No one will ever enter Heaven without Eternal Life. Nothing but God-life can exist there. He who has *that* Life will be admitted. He who has not will be barred.

This was Christ's purpose in coming to the world. "I am come that they might have Life," He declared (John 10: 10).

Why is Eternal Life necessary? Because men are "dead in trespasses and sins" (Eph. 2: 1, 5). Man is a triune being, composed of spirit, soul, and body. What was it that died when Adam fell? God's pronouncement was: "In the day thou eatest thereof thou shalt surely die." What died? Was it his body? Certainly not, not that day. Physically he was as much alive as ever. Was it his soul—his intellect and emotions? By no means. He was still able to think, plan and feel. Then it must have been his spirit. Until that day his fellowship with God had been unbroken. But from the very hour he sinned he was out of touch with God. Hence it is the spirit that must be quickened into life.

Men may appear to be alive simply because soul and body are both active. But as God looks down upon the human race He divides men into two classes only—the quick and the dead. You are at this moment in one or the other.

We look at a man walking down the street, and we say: "That man is certainly alive." What do we mean? Why, simply that his body is alive. He possesses physical life. But his spirit may be dead, and, if so—if he has never been born again—then in God's sight he is dead.

We watch a keen businessman at work in his office and we say: "There is a live man for you." But what do we mean? Merely that his soulish nature is alive. His intellect is active, his emotions are responsive. But God looks at him and gives a very different verdict: "He is dead," He says. You see, we speak of temporal life, but God of eternal.

We attend the funeral of a Christian and view the remains. So far as we are concerned, the man is dead. By that we mean that his body is dead. But God says: "He is alive." You see, he had been quickened in his spirit; he had received Eternal Life and thereby had been born anew. Hence, though soul and body are pronounced dead, he is alive.

Determines Man's Destiny

Moreover, it determines man's eternal destiny. "He that believeth on the Son hath Everlasting Life: and he that believeth not the Son shall not see Life; but the wrath of God abideth on him" (John 3: 36). On one side, Life. On the other side, "the wrath of God".

"Verily, verily, I say unto you, he that heareth my word, and believeth on Him that sent me, hath Everlasting Life, and shall not come into condemnation; but is passed from death unto Life" (John 5: 24). Here again are the two sides—Life or condemnation.

"I give unto them Eternal Life; and they shall never perish" (John 10: 28). To reject the gift of Life is to perish. You must make the choice. Man chooses his own destiny.

Do you, my friend, possess Eternal Life or do you not? Upon the answer to this question depends your eternal happiness or woe.

Birth and Life

Now apart from birth there can be no life. Natural or physical life enters the world through birth and so does spiritual. "Ye must be born again." Christ must enter your heart, and the moment He does, Life, Eternal Life, is yours.

Oh my friend, Christianity is not a dead, cold, formal belief. Christianity is a Life, the Life of God in the heart of man. That is what makes it unique.

Our parents gave us natural birth but God gives us spiritual birth, for natural birth is not sufficient. To be born once is to die twice, but to be born twice is to die but once.

Only spiritual birth makes God our father. "Ye are of your father the devil" (John 8: 44), said Jesus. God is your Creator but not your father. There is no such thing as the universal fatherhood of God and the universal brotherhood of man. You are not my brother until you have been born into the family of which I am a member, the family of God, and only then is God your Father.

A Radical Change

When you are born again there is a radical change: "If any man be in Christ he is a new creature (creation), old things are passed away: behold, all things are become new" (2 Cor. 5: 17). Apart from this change there is no life. When Christ enters, all things become new. Otherwise it is a spurious conversion. The things you once loved you now hate and the things you once hated you love.

From Death to Life

To be born again means to pass out of death and into Life. You do not enter the spiritual world at death. When death comes you pass from one condition of that world to another. It is still the same world. The really great change takes place at conversion. All men are born in the natural world. The spiritual is another sphere altogether. All efforts at self-improvement can only end within the circle of the natural. There must come a life from the spiritual world, entirely outside the natural, and that life must enter the heart, thereby translating you from the natural world to the spiritual.

You enter the Kingdom of God while here. At death you simply enter a different compartment of the same kingdom. Every man living is at this moment in one world or the other. He is in the kingdom of darkness or the Kingdom of Light, the kingdom of Satan or the Kingdom of God. In which are you?

I often think of the acorn and the diamond; the acorn dull and unattractive, the diamond sparkling in all its brilliancy. And many a church member, like the acorn, is dull and unattractive as a Christian, while many an unsaved worldly man prides himself on his morality and boasts of how much better he is than the church member he knows, and rightly so. He resembles the diamond.

But let us plant them and seventy-five years later return to the spot. What do we find? There where the acorn was placed is a lordly oak, strong and straight, well able to withstand the storms that beat against it. Now dig down in the spot where the diamond was buried, and lo! there is nothing but a diamond. What made the difference? Why, one had life, the other did not.

And so it is with the natural man and the spiritual man; the one has Life, Eternal Life, but the other is lifeless. The spiritual man has the Life of God and will live with Him in Eternity; the moral man, though outwardly attractive, is nevertheless dead. He does not possess the one great essential, namely, Life. And so morality is not sufficient; it is void of Life. Nicodemus was both moral and religious, but Jesus said to him: "Ye must be born again."

Here are two bouquets of flowers. At a distance both are equally beautiful. But upon closer scrutiny a vast difference is discernible. From one there arises a most exquisite perfume. But from the other—nothing. It is found to be artificial, a manufactured imitation of the real thing. One is alive, the other dead. One has life, the other is lifeless.

And so it is with you. But imitation, profession, appearance will not do. To be like a Christian is not to be one. To profess is one thing; to possess is another. Artificial salvation is not salvation. No painted hypocrite, however perfect, will pass. To have God's nature you must possess God's Life.

Christianity is not merely a system of ethics or a moral code; it is the implantation of a new Life; the Life of God in the heart of man, by the operation of the Holy Spirit. Obedience to the Sermon on the Mount, along with all the other moral teachings of the Bible, would not produce Life. "He that hath the Son hath Life, and he that hath not the Son of God hath not Life" (1 John 5: 12).

A New Species

The new birth involves a new species. "That which is born of the flesh is flesh." You can never cross the species. Men have tried but have failed. They have obtained new varieties, but not new species. This is one of the unchangeable laws of God. Animal is always animal. Fish have never been changed into birds. But "that which is born of the Spirit is spirit". Here now is a different species, and it is only when men have been born of the Spirit of God that they receive this new nature.

Why is it that you act as you do? Why do you sin? Because of what you are. You do what you do because you are what you are. If you are in Adam you will do what he did. If you are in Christ you will do what He does. I am a Smith because I was born into the family of Smiths. I look like my father. I walk like my father. Not because I try to, not because I want to imitate him, but simply because I am a Smith. I was born into the family.

Why do dogs bark, roosters crow and cats meow? They never took lessons. Nobody ever taught them. They do what they do in a perfectly natural way. You have never yet heard a dog meow or a cat bark. Why not? A dog, because it was born into the family of dogs, barks. A rooster crows for the same reason, and cats meow because they are cats. These are the families to which they belong. They do what they do because they are what they are.

Have you ever watched cows and horses get up? How does a cow get up? If you have lived on a farm, you know. Cows always get up on their hind legs first. But you never saw a horse get up on its hind legs. Horses get up on their front legs. Why the difference? Just because it is their nature.

Our nature is to sin, and until we receive a new nature within, we will continue to sin. Our old nature will manifest itself. It could not be otherwise. The new birth means a new nature and we will never act differently until we have been born again and have received that new nature. Hence the absolute necessity of the new birth.

Do you know that only God-life can exist in Heaven? Natural life has no place there. The life given to a fish is the life that enables it to live under water. The life of a bird permits it to exist in the air. The Life of God is the only life that is suitable for Heaven. Hence Jesus did not make an arbitrary statement when He said: "Ye must be born again." He was simply announcing a fact. If a man is to live in Heaven he must have a nature suitable for Heaven.

A Present Experience

Moreover, it is a present experience. "He that believeth on the Son HATH everlasting life" (John 3: 36). "Verily, verily, I say unto you, he that heareth my word, and believeth on Him that sent me, HATH everlasting life, and shall not come into condemnation; but is passed from death unto life" (John 5: 24). "He that hath the Son HATH Life" (1 John 5: 12). Thank God, you can be saved NOW.

The early Methodist preachers were called the "now" preachers because they offered salvation on the spot. It is not something to be received at death or after death; it is something that is received *now*. If you do not possess this Life before you die, you will never possess it. "Now is the accepted time; behold, now is the day of salvation."

An Instantaneous Experience

Again it is an instantaneous experience. It must be. Birth is always a crisis, and spiritual birth is no exception. It does not take a year to be born. That is why we have birthdays. Every one of us can point to some definite day when he was born. So, too, the new birth must be a crisis experience. It may take a long time to get to it, but when it happens it happens suddenly.

If you will examine each and every case of conversion you will find that every one was instantaneous—the 3,000 on the day of Pentecost, Paul on the road to Damascus, the Philippian jailer—all were instantaneously converted.

How else could it be? Suppose I offer you a gift. There is a moment when you do not have it. The next moment you have it. The gift must have been transferred from my hand to your hand instantaneously. Eternal Life is a gift. There is a time when you do not possess it. There is a time when you do. There must be a moment when you accept it. It could not be otherwise. There is no known case of gradual conversion. Life is always instantaneously received.

A Knowable Experience

Then, too, it is a knowable experience. "These things have I written unto you that ye may know that ye have Eternal Life" (1 John 5: 13). Not that ye may hope or guess, but that ye may K-N-O-W—*KNOW*.

Years ago when I was a missionary to the Indians, a worker from one of our most prominent denominations heard me say that I knew I was saved. She thought I was most presumptuous. "Do you not know?" I asked. "Certainly not," was her answer. "I cannot possibly know until the Judgment Day."

I looked at her in amazement. "And yet you have come out here to be a missionary to the Indians; you are going to urge them to become Christians and you do not know whether you yourself are a Christian."

Isn't it strange that we are positive about everything else except this. Suppose I ask you such questions as these: "Are you married? Have you children? Have you had your dinner?" You do not answer, "I think so. I hope so." You answer definitely either "Yes" or "No". Yet when it comes to salvation you hesitate.

Indestructible

Finally, it is indestructible. Some day you will hear that Oswald Smith is dead. Don't you believe it. At that moment I will be more alive than ever, for I have an indestructible life.

The man who has Eternal Life, God says, shall "not die. He shall live forever" (John 6: 50–51). "Whosoever liveth and believeth in me shall never die" (John 11: 26), said Jesus. Again and again the Bible speaks of "Everlasting Life, Eternal Life". Jesus has "abolished death" (2 Tim. 1: 10).

Men may destroy my body, but they cannot kill me. They may damage the house in which I live, but I am immortal. Cut off my arms if you will, but I am still alive. Sever my legs, but still I live. Take off my head and what have you done? You have damaged my dwelling, but you have not touched me.

You have released me from my prison. I can now go on living in a new world, a life of freedom and joy that I have never known before. You have opened my cage and let me out. No longer do I have to drag a tired, weak and sickly body around with me. I am now free.

My Text

"God hath given to us Eternal Life, and this Life is in His Son. He that hath the Son hath Life; and he that hath not the Son of God hath not Life" (1 John 5: 11–12).

"God hath given." Salvation is a gift. You cannot earn it, work for it, or merit it. As a matter of fact you cannot get it unless you are willing to accept it as a gift. "The gift of God is Eternal Life through Jesus Christ our Lord" (Rom. 6: 23). You must come as a pauper. You must take it as you would a Christmas gift.

Did the prodigal son have anything to pay or offer in return for his father's kindness? Did he pay anything for the shoes, the robe, the ring and the fatted calf? No, indeed! So it is with Eternal Life.

"God hath given to us Eternal Life." Suppose this piece of paper represents Eternal Life. Now listen: "God hath given to us Eternal Life, and this Life is in His Son." I take this piece of paper. I put it in this book. And just as the paper is in the book, so Eternal Life is in Christ. It is not in the Church, it is not in morality, it is not in religion, it is in Christ. Unless, therefore, you come to Christ you will never get it, for you will never find it except in Him.

Now listen to the next statement: "He that hath the Son hath Life." If I have this book, I also have this paper. If I want the paper I will have to go to the book for it, for that is where it is. God has placed Eternal Life in His Son, and now He says: "He that hath the Son hath Life." Therefore you do not have to worry about Eternal Life; you only have to ask yourself one question: "Is Jesus Christ, God's Son, my Saviour?" If I have the Son I have Life.

Now note the last statement: "But he that hath *not* the Son of God hath not Life." There is no Life apart from Christ. If I do not have Christ I do not have Life, and if I do not have Life I am lost.

Why then will you perish? Jesus gives the answer: "Ye *will not* come to Me that ye might have Life" (John 5: 40). Not ye *cannot* but ye *will not*. Hence if you are to have Eternal Life, the greatest gift ever offered, you must come to Jesus. You must receive Him as your own personal Saviour. Will you do it? Do it, and do it—NOW.

CHAPTER IX

WHEN THE HARVEST IS PAST

YEARS ago, when I was in my later teens, soon after I was converted, I was attending a Bible Class in Chalmer's Presbyterian Church, Toronto. During the session I happened to hear a group of men discussing a new pastor who had just taken over a church on King Street—St. Mark's Presbyterian, by name. They told about the wonderful crowds he was gathering and of his evangelistic ministry. His name, so I learned, was Rev J. D. Morrow, an athlete who had won many a trophy as a runner.

Immediately I was all attention. Something in my young heart responded to what I had heard, and I made up my mind that I would lose no time in attending a service and hearing Mr. Morrow for myself.

On Sunday night I found myself in St. Mark's. The auditorium was rapidly filling. There was great excitement on every side. I could feel it in the very atmosphere. Before long, the church was filled to capacity. Presently Mr. Morrow stepped out and took charge. He wore his hair long. As a matter of fact, it was right down on his shoulders. He had a smile on his face, and as I watched him I realized that I was looking upon a leader of men, a man who could accomplish great things for God.

The singing was evangelistic in character. The old gospel songs were used. Mr. Morrow himself led them.

The entire service was bright and cheerful and most attractive. My young heart immediately responded.

But that which held my attention more than anything else was the message. Mr. Morrow took as his text Jeremiah 8: 20—"The harvest is past, the summer is ended, and we are not saved." And then, with pleading voice, he commenced appealing to his congregation to decide for Jesus Christ. Never will I forget that appeal, and although many, many years have passed, I can still remember it. My heart was gripped, and as he spoke my eyes were fixed upon him. His voice was tender and appealing. The entire audience sat in perfect silence, listening to every word.

Again and again he repeated the words of his text—"The harvest is past, the summer is ended, and we are not saved." There was an atmosphere about it that I have never forgotten. I was listening to a man who was dead in earnest, a man who felt every word that he uttered. He spoke as a dying man to dying men, laying bare the souls of those before him, pleading, entreating, beseeching.

Little did Mr. Morrow know that his successor, a young man only eighteen years of age, was listening to him that night. Mr. Morrow's every word stirred me as I had never been stirred before. I took to him at once. Here was a man I could follow, a man who could lead me as I desired to be led, a man whose message inspired me. It is a long time since that wonderful night, but the text still rings in my ears, and I still hear the pleading tones of the preacher, who long since has gone to his reward—"The harvest is past, the summer is ended, and we are not saved."

There is a hymn that I used to hear when I was quite young. It was sung in the days of D. L. Moody and was often used in evangelistic meetings, though it is found in very few hymn books today. The chorus of it went like this:

When the harvest is past,
And the summer is o'er,
And Jesus invites thee no more.

That Gospel song still lingers with me, though it is over a quarter of a century now since I have heard it sung in public. It is a hymn that has been much used to bring souls to Christ, a hymn of warning and admonition. It tells of a harvest and it warns that a day will come when the harvest will be past, and the summer will end. It brings conviction and a realization of the nearness of Eternity and the danger of delay.

Now there are four things that I want to say in connection with the harvest and each one is of paramount importance. Let me enumerate them, one by one.

First—There is Always a Time of Harvest

When I was a boy at Embro, I used to see train-loads of harvesters hurrying to the Western Provinces of Canada. This occurred every year as regular as clockwork, and it made a deep impression upon me. It only lasted for a matter of a couple of weeks, but while it did last there was great excitement.

Special harvest trains stopped at our station day after day, and groups of men boarded them. I was told that they were going to Manitoba, Saskatchewan and Alberta, in order to gather in the great wheat harvest that was now ripe and ready to be reaped, and that if they did not go at once it would be lost.

Now why the hurry? Why was it that they could not go at some other time? Why must it always be at the same time each year? Simply because, unless they hurried to the West and garnered in the harvest, that harvest would be lost, and lost forever. Hence, there was no time to lose. It was now or never.

My friends, let me say that exactly the same is true of

the great spiritual harvest. It, too, must be garnered in. There are times when God's Spirit is actively at work in a community, when the Gospel is being preached and souls are being saved, when the Holy Spirit is convicting men of their need of Christ. There are times of special visitation when decisions are being made, and to miss such opportunities is to run the risk of being lost, and lost eternally.

All down through the centuries there have been such times. There was a special day of visitation during the lifetime of Noah. You remember, he preached for a hundred and twenty years, warning men of a coming flood and urging them to escape from the wrath of God. But they ignored his warnings. They would not heed. Never had they seen rain. They could not conceive of such a judgment. So they laughed and mocked. But Noah went right on preaching—preaching and building, while the multitudes, even including the carpenters who worked for him, ignored his warnings and ridiculed his words.

The people had been living in sin. They had turned away from God. Immorality, corruption, violence and brutality characterized their civilization, and these things God has always abhorred. But in spite of the awful corruption and violence on every side, God gave them an opportunity to repent.

Suddenly, the predicted judgment came and they were overwhelmed. The rain descended, the waters rose higher and higher. Finally, every mountain was covered. Noah and his family were safe in the ark and the door was shut. All the others were on the outside, and, being outside the ark, they were drowned in the waters of the flood.

There was another day of visitation. It had to do with Judah and Israel. Prophet after prophet was sent. The people were warned. They were given every possible opportunity. It did not happen suddenly. There were generations when God sent His servants to warn them of the coming captivity, but they would not heed. They went on in their sin and rebellion, ignoring God's prophets and their warnings. At last the judgment fell. Samaria was taken, then Jerusalem, and the people carried away into captivity. Famine raged in the cities. Women ate their own children. Blood flowed on every side. Terrible indeed was the judgment. The harvest had passed.

There was another day of visitation. It was when Jesus was here. He, too, warned of impending judgment, but His words fell on deaf ears. "O Jerusalem, Jerusalem," He cried, "thou that killest the prophets, and stonest them which are sent unto thee, how often would I have gathered thy children together, even as a hen gathereth her chickens under her wings, and ye would not! Behold, your house is left unto you desolate" (Matt. 23: 37–38).

In A.D. 70 the judgment fell, and, oh, how terrible it was! What suffering, what tribulation, what anguish of heart. The streets of the city flowed in blood. Thousands of crosses lined the highways, until, as Josephus tells us, they looked like a forest, each one with a dying victim hanging on it. Cannibalism held the city in its grip. Then came the world-wide dispersion—a dispersion that has continued to this very hour, and all because the people would not recognize God's day of visitation and turn from their sins. Once again the harvest passed, the summer ended, and they were not saved. Oh, what a calamity!

We, too, have had a visitation. Never in the history of the world has there been so much Gospel preaching as during our generation. Think, if you will, of the evangelism of the last hundred years, or more. England was on the brink of ruin, headed for the French Revolution, when God raised up John Wesley, George Whitfield and Charles Wesley, and sent them out to preach the Gospel.

That was the greatest visitation the world has ever seen since the days of the apostles. There never has been anything like it either before or since. Wesley's evangelists went all over the world, not as pastors but as flaming revivalists, to preach the Gospel and win souls to Jesus Christ. Methodism was used of God to warn men everywhere and to urge upon them the necessity of conversion.

Then we had a Finney and Moody in America, under whose ministry God sent revival and evangelism the like of which America had never known before. Thousands upon thousands were saved; but many, even then, rejected God's offer of mercy and ignored His visitation.

Then God sent Spurgeon, Sunday, Torrey, Gipsy Smith, and they, too, urged upon the people the necessity of repentance and called the multitudes to turn and accept Christ. That, too, was a day of visitation when God spoke to perishing men and women everywhere, but even then countless thousands ignored His appeal.

And now in these latter days we have a Billy Graham crying to the nation to get right with God or face judgment. Never once has God left Himself without witnesses. Always before judgment He has offered mercy. But it must be one or the other—either mercy or judgment. It cannot be both. If you, my friend, will not accept the mercy of God, in this your day of visitation, then you must face His judgment.

SECOND—APART FROM GOD THERE CAN BE NO HARVEST

I want to make it perfectly clear that man has very little to do with it. Man can plant and water, but only God gives the increase. There are those who preach and teach—those who warn and exhort, those who plead and implore. There are those who do all that can be done to urge men to be reconciled to God. But after man has done his utmost, it remains with God to give the increase. Only God can save men after all.

Do you remember the words of the Lord Jesus in John 6: 44? He said, "No man can come to me, except the

Father which hath sent me draw him." My friend, that is one of the most serious statements to be found in the Word of God. You think you can be saved whenever you want to. You have an idea that you can accept Christ when you are ready. I want to say that you can do nothing of the kind. You must accept Jesus Christ during the day of visitation, when the Holy Spirit is at work in your heart.

Now, let me ask you, have you ever felt the wooings of the Holy Spirit? Has God ever drawn you to Himself? Has there ever been a desire in your heart to accept Jesus Christ as your personal Saviour? Can you remember a time when you wanted to be saved—when you longed to be born again? Have you ever been burdened about the salvation of your soul? Do you know anything about the convicting power of the Holy Spirit?

My friend, if you have, then you have been conscious of the voice of God. God Himself has been speaking to you. The Holy Spirit has been urging you to turn and be saved. That was the time you should have made your decision. Perhaps now your heart is hard, cold and indifferent. Perhaps now you have no desire to be converted. It may be that the conviction has worn off, the Spirit has left you, and God has turned away.

Not because He wanted to; God never gives men up until they give Him up. But if you have persisted in ignoring the wooings of the Holy Spirit, and have refused to be reconciled to God, it may be that the desire has gone. Every time you refuse, it is harder the next time. Every time you say no, it is more difficult to say yes.

I say again, there is a time when God's Spirit visits you, when there is a movement of the Holy Ghost, when God draws near and you are conscious of His pleadings. He alone can save your soul and unless He does it never will be done, for apart from God there can be no harvest. Therefore, "Today, if ye will hear His voice, harden not your hearts" (Heb. 4: 7).

If you, my friend, ignore His time of visitation, you may find it impossible to come. I urge you, therefore, to examine your own heart and to ask yourself whether or not the Holy Spirit is dealing with you, whether or not there is any desire to be saved, whether or not you are anxious about your soul's salvation, whether or not God is still drawing you to Himself, for again I say, apart from God there can be no harvest. "No man can come to me, except the Father which hath sent me draw him."

Third—The Harvest is Always Gathered in its Prime

Do you realize that very few people are ever saved after they are thirty years of age, and that most of them are saved before they are twenty-five? As a matter of fact, whenever I have tested an audience, I have discovered that the vast majority were saved in their teens. My friend, that is a very solemn fact. If only a few are saved after they are thirty, if the vast majority are saved before, then what about you? Are you over thirty? If you are, then your chances are slim.

It is when the harvest is ripe that it is garnered in. It must be in its prime. It is when young men and women are on the threshold of life, that the Spirit of God moves mightily upon them. Then if they resist and become hardened, little by little, it becomes more difficult until, at last, as middle life and old age creep on, they find their hearts unresponsive, and they discover that they belong to those who accept Christ—not in multitudes, but in ones and twos.

It may be that they become hardened by sin. Habits become fixed. In the early years they are easy to break, but once the thread has been wound around and around, it becomes difficult to break. Do you remember how you felt the first time you sinned, and then do you remember what happened later on? You became accustomed to your sin, did you not?

At first there was terrible conviction. Your conscience troubled you, but you did not listen. You went on and on until at last you could commit the sin and your conscience scarcely spoke to you at all. All you have to do is to turn over and refuse to listen to the alarm clock once too often and the next time you will not even hear it ring. So it is with sin. It gets a hold on you until at last it has mastered you. Conscience is silenced. The alarm no longer rings—at least you do not hear it.

Thus you go on in your sin and the Spirit of God is ignored. When sin gets a grip on you, you cannot give it up; you become its slave and it becomes your master. Then when you have successfully silenced conscience and quenched the Holy Spirit, you continue in your rebellion, and as you grow older and older it becomes increasingly difficult to right-about-face and accept Jesus Christ.

My friend, what about it? Are you in the prime of life? Are you still young? Are you yet in your teens? Then why not accept the Lord Jesus Christ now before it is forever too late? Or are you already over thirty years of age and will you soon be in your forties? Then beware. Your chances are poor. You will find it more difficult with every year that passes. No wonder God said, "Now is the accepted time; behold, now is the day of salvation" (2 Cor. 6:2).

FOURTH—THE HARVEST ALWAYS COMES TO AN END

Yes, at last, "the harvest is past, the summer is ended." And are you among those of whom it will be said, "and we are not saved"? How dreadful! Do you know what happens to the grain that is not garnered in? It is left out in the field and destroyed. Will that be your doom? Are you going to be lost? Must you perish? What a tragedy!

Listen to me, my friend. If there are no more strivings

of the Spirit of God, then for you the harvest is past. If the revival has ended and you are still unsaved, then for you, I say, the harvest is past. If you are no longer troubled, if you are unconcerned, if you have become indifferent, then again I say, for you the harvest is past. If the Spirit no longer pleads, if God no longer entreats, if your heart is cold and hard, then the harvest for you, I say, is past.

Do you remember the Word of God? "My Spirit shall not always strive with man," He says. Yes, there comes a time when God's Spirit ceases to strive, because you have resisted all His strivings. You have vexed His Holy Spirit, for in spite of all He has done you have not come. For you, I say, the harvest is past and the summer is ended. It may now be too late.

But, my friend, it need not be too late. If you take Christ and take Him now, it will not be too late. But if you do not, then you will some day find yourself among those who will cry out, "The harvest is past, the summer is ended, and we are not saved."

Will that be your fate? It need not be. But it will, if you go on as you are. "He, that being often reproved hardeneth his neck, shall suddenly be destroyed, and that without remedy" (Prov. 29: 1). Oh then, come. "Put your trust in the Lord Jesus, and you will be saved" (Acts 16: 31, N.E.B.). Will you do it? Do it, and do it—NOW.

CHAPTER X

FIVE SOLEMN FACTS

THERE are *five solemn facts* with which I want to deal, facts of such vital importance that to ignore them is to wilfully reject the warning of God's infallible Word, and deliberately disregard the danger signals of divine truth. Therefore, beware! Eternal issues are at stake.

First: All Will Not Be Saved

There is no such thing as universal salvation; some will be saved, others—lost. Make no mistake, let no one deceive you—a day of separation is surely coming, a separation of the wheat from the tares, the good from the bad, the sheep from the goats. On one side or the other, every man and woman will be arraigned. I care not what the Universalists say, such is the solemn declaration of Scripture over and over again; and the question is, Will you be among the saved or the lost?

All I have to do in order to substantiate the statement I have made is to refer you to the parables of the wheat and the tares, and the dragnet. We cannot argue over the interpretation because the Lord Himself explains them. The wheat, He tells us, represents the children of God, the tares the children of Satan.

The servants wanted to go and root out the tares, leaving only the wheat. But He said, "Let both grow together until the harvest; and in the time of harvest I will say to the reapers, Gather ye together first the tares, and bind them in bundles to burn them: but gather the wheat into my barn" (Matt. 13: 30).

How long were they to grow together? Until the harvest. When will the harvest be? At the end of the age. That means then that there will be tares as well as wheat in the field when the age ends, children of Satan as well as children of God. If all are to be saved then all the tares must become wheat. But that does not happen. The tares remain tares. The tares are not to be saved; they are to be gathered into bundles and burned.

The same is true of the dragnet. It gathers of all, both good and bad alike. Now there are bad fish in the sea. But this is the Kingdom net, this is the visible Church, and lo and behold, there are bad fish in the net itself. Nor will there be any separation until the age ends. Only then will the good be separated from the bad. Hence all will not be saved.

"The Son of man shall send forth His angels, and they shall gather out of His kingdom all things that offend, and them which do iniquity; and shall cast them into the furnace of fire . . . Then shall the righteous shine forth as the sun in the kingdom of their Father" (Matt 13: 41–43).

"The angels shall come forth and sever the wicked from among the just" (Matt. 13: 49).

"He shall separate them one from another, as a shepherd divideth *his* sheep from the goats; and He shall set the sheep on His right hand, but the goats on the left. Then shall the King say unto them on His right hand, Come, ye blessed of my Father, inherit the kingdom prepared for you from the foundation of the world. Then shall He say also unto them on the left hand, Depart from me, ye cursed, into everlasting fire, prepared for the devil and his angels. And these shall go away into everlasting punishment, but the righteous into life eternal" (Matt. 25: 32–34, 41, 46).

The angels, our Lord says, will sever the wicked from

the just. He will put the sheep on His right hand and the goats on His left. To the one he will say, "Come, ye blessed", to the other, "Depart, ye cursed". Hence, if there is to be a separation, all will not be saved. And again I ask: Will you be among the saved or among the lost?

Second: The Majority Will Be Lost

"Wide is the gate, and broad is the way that leadeth to destruction, and *many* there be which go in thereat." Many does not mean few. Many means many. "Strait is the gate, and narrow is the way which leadeth unto life, and *few* there be that find it." Few does not mean many. Few means few. There will be many on the broad way and few on the narrow (Matt. 7: 13–14).

"But how can a God of love," you exclaim, "consign the majority to perdition? Surely the majority will be saved, and only a very few, the great outstanding sinners of the centuries, lost." No, my friend, the majority will be lost.

Let me ask you this question: Was there ever a time when this God of love of whom you speak did allow the majority to be lost? There was. It was at the time of the flood. Only eight were saved. All the others perished, the good and the bad, the old and the young, little new-born babes—all perished beneath the waters of the flood.

If God did it once, is it not conceivable that He might do it again? He did do it again. Do you remember Sodom and Gomorrah? How many escaped? Only three. All the others perished. If, therefore, God did it a second time He might do it a third time. He will do it a third time. We know perfectly well that the vast majority will reject Jesus Christ and be lost.

Why, even today, the broad way is thronged while the narrow way is trodden by but few. Think of heathenism if you will, China's seven hundred millions,

India's five hundred millions, France and Southern Europe. The overwhelming majority have no knowledge whatever of the Gospel.

"Yes," you say, "but what about America, Christian America? Surely in America the majority will be found on the narrow way." Is that so? Let me tell you that one half of the people of America never darken a church door, let alone call themselves Christians.

If you will visit all the churches of a given city on a Sunday evening, when everyone should be in church, and if you will count the number present, and then subtract it from the total population, you will find the vast majority outside the churches and only a few, comparatively speaking, inside. Test it and see. The majority do not travel the narrow way. With which are you? This is one time when I want to be with the minority.

THIRD: MANY WILL PERISH WHO EXPECT TO BE SAVED

This is the saddest fact of all. Multitudes who confidently expect to be in Heaven, will awaken when it is too late, to find that they have never been born again. All their lifetime they have been deceived. Satan has kept the scales on their eyes to the very last, and, finally, when it is too late, the scales fall off and they realize that they have never been saved. Oh, awful thought!—to be on a false foundation, unsaved, self-deceived, and lost eternally. Profession without possession, and the door of mercy closed. Then, alas, the bitter cry will be, "Too late! Too late!"

According to God's Word one builds his house on rock, another on sand. One looks just as attractive as the other. And as long as the sun is shining, one appears to be as secure as the other. But suddenly the storm breaks, and the house on the rock withstands the blast, while the one on the sand falls. So will it be in that day. Many who think they have built well will find their foundations giving way and will perish. Are you, my friend, on the solid rock Christ Jesus, or are you on the sinking sand of your own works? I am so glad I am able to say:

On Christ the solid rock I stand,
All other ground is sinking sand.

"Not every one that saith unto me, Lord, Lord, shall enter into the kingdom of heaven. Many will say to me in that day, Lord, Lord, have we not prophesied in Thy name and in Thy name have cast out devils, and in Thy name done many wonderful works? And then will I profess unto them, I never knew you. Depart from me ye that work iniquity" (Matt. 7: 21–27).

Oh, my brother, my sister, can it be possible that this will be *your* fatal doom? Has Satan blinded *your* eyes; are *you* deceived? *You* who *have* listened to the Gospel all your life; *you* who have been brought up in a Christian home, and trained in the Sunday School; *you* who have been an active member of the church—tell me, are *you* resting on a false foundation; and will *you* discover when it is too late that *you* were never saved at all? For, remember, *many will perish who expect to be saved,* and *you* may be among the number.

Fourth: There is No Salvation After Death

We read in God's Word of a great gulf. We are told two things about this gulf. First, it is fixed. That means it can never be moved. It is permanent. Second, it is impassable. No one can cross from one side to the other.

This means that there is no second chance, in spite of what Jehovah's Witnesses say. If you, my friend, die unsaved, you will remain unsaved. The Bible does not offer a glimmer of hope to anyone who rejects Christ in this life. There is no hope beyond the grave, no second chance.

Why should there be? If you deliberately refuse to accept Jesus Christ now, why should God offer you another opportunity in the life to come? What is there in death that would change you? If you are against God now you will be against Him then. You may be sorry for your sufferings, but you will not reverse your decision. If you do not want to be saved now, you will not want to be saved hereafter.

Suppose you offer me a Christmas gift, and I spurn your offer and hurl your gift back into your face. Would you come around next Christmas and offer me another gift? Well, you might if you loved me enough. But suppose I should take your second gift and trample it under foot, telling you that I did not want it, would you return the third time with a similar offer? I think not.

Yet you have an idea that in spite of the number of times you reject Jesus Christ, God's mercy should never be exhausted. He should return again and again and give you another, and still another chance. How absurd. Why should He? I want to warn you that there is a day coming when He will never again renew His offer. If you, my friend, go out of this life without Christ, you will never accept Him. You will be lost and lost forever, for there is no salvation after death.

Fifth: This May Be Your Last Opportunity

"Yes, I would like to be a Christian, and intend to be sometime," said a man to his friend one day, "but I want to enjoy the pleasures of the world first."

"Well, that's all right," responded his friend. "Go on and enjoy the world! You can become a Christian afterwards."

"But just when should I become a Christian?" inquired the other, in a somewhat anxious tone of voice.

"Oh, *five minutes before you die* will be time enough," replied his friend in a casual sort of way.

"But I don't know *when* I am going to die," he exclaimed. "I may not have another five minutes to live."

"In that case," remarked his friend, "the time to become a Christian is *now*."

"Boast not thyself of tomorrow; for thou knowest not what a day may bring forth" (Prov. 27: 1). You may have another chance but, remember, there is a time coming when you will not, when you will have to make the final choice. And this, my unsaved friend, may be that time. As sure as God lives, the hour will strike when you will attend your last meeting, hear your last sermon, and make your last choice.

Remember, there is no "tomorrow" with God. His Word declares that "*now* is the accepted time; behold, *now* is the day of salvation" (2 Cor. 6: 2). God's time is *now*.

"Why," you ask, "may this be my last opportunity?"

First: Because Life Is Uncertain

One night in The Peoples Church I concluded my service as usual and pronounced the benediction. A young woman had been sitting in the gallery in front of me but she hadn't responded to the invitation. At the close of the service I got into my car and drove along Bloor Street to Bay. There I saw a great crowd, several policemen and two or three street cars. Parking my car, I walked over to the corner, and there under the wheels of one of the street cars I saw the body of the young woman who had been sitting before me in the gallery ten minutes earlier, almost every bone in her body broken —dead.

Did she know that she would never hear another sermon, that she would never have another opportunity? Why, of course not. She expected to be back next Sunday night as usual. She thought she had lots of time. But for her it was the end. She would never have an opportunity again.

Do you remember the rich man? Did he know that he would never see another sunrise, that that night would be his last? Of course not. He went to bed having made wonderful plans for the future, and looking forward to executing every one of them. But in the dead of night he heard the voice of God. "Thou fool," He said, "this night thy soul shall be required of thee."

I didn't call this man a fool. God did. When is a man a fool? When he makes ample provision for this life, but none for the next. That was what this man did. He prepared for the present, but not for the future. Hence God called him a fool. He had had his last opportunity.

Oh, fool, fool, not to reckon with the uncertainty of life! And will you, too, play the fool, and continue to procrastinate until suddenly your doom is sealed? Why, man, the next train you ride on may hurl you into the presence of your Maker! The street you cross on your way home may see your mangled body beneath the wheels of a passing car. Yea, even now, while plans for to-morrow are passing through your mind, the voice of God, could you but hear it, may be saying to you also, "Thou fool, *this night* thy soul shall be required of thee," or "This year thou shalt die" (Jer. 28: 16).

Second: Because Jesus Is Coming

When He will come I do not know, but I do know that He is coming back, and when He returns it will mean judgment for the unsaved. Again and again He said, when He was on earth: "Be ye also ready, for in such an hour as ye think not, the Son of Man cometh."

Are you, my friend, ready? Would you like Him to return tonight? Would you welcome Him, or would you be ashamed before Him? Would you want to call on the rocks and the mountains to fall on you and hide you from His face? Does the thought of His coming strike terror into your heart?

"We which are alive," says Paul, "will be caught up to meet the Lord in the air." Would you be caught up, or would you be left behind? You do not know when He will return, and, remember, it is to be sudden, in the twinkling of an eye, and there will be no time to prepare. Therefore, I say, this may be your last opportunity, because Jesus may come.

Third: Because the Spirit May Cease to Strive

"God is departed from me." Those were the saddest words Saul ever uttered. It is a terrible thing when your wife departs from you, or your child. But when God departs, there is no hope. Let me say, however, that God never departs until you depart. God will not leave you until you leave Him.

"God gave them up." Those were the words of the apostle Paul. It is an awful thing to have your father give you up, or to have your husband give you up. But when God gives you up you are indeed hopeless. I must again state, however, that God does not give you up until you give Him up. But when He does, there is no hope. You will have had your last opportunity.

There is an unpardonable sin, a sin that even God Himself cannot forgive. That sin is the final rejection of the Lord Jesus Christ. Last Sunday night you said "No" when the invitation was given. Tonight you are going to say "No" again. One of these nights you will say "No" for the last time. It may be tonight. I do not know. You do not know. Only God knows.

But if this should be your last opportunity, and if you are going to say "No" tonight, for the last time, then you will never have a chance again, for you will have committed the unpardonable sin. You will come back next Sunday night, and you will enjoy the service as usual. But when the invitation is given, you will have no desire to accept Christ. "My Spirit shall not always strive with man" (Gen. 6: 3).

Too Late!

D. L. Moody had a class of young men. He had won most of them to Christ, but one had refused to yield. One day he spoke to him, urging him to make his decision.

"Listen, Mr. Moody," replied the young man, "I'm going west, and after I have made my fortune, when I return, I promise you I will accept Christ," and he turned away.

Mr. Moody listened with a sad heart. Some weeks later the young man became seriously ill and was taken to the hospital. Mr. Moody felt led to visit him, and bending over his bed he again urged him to accept Jesus Christ. But once more, this time in a feeble voice, he refused.

"Mr. Moody," he said, "I'm not going to die. I'm going to get better, and, as I told you before, I'm going west, and when I come back I'll become a Christian." Mr. Moody turned away with a heavy heart.

Finally, one day, the young man, who did get better, came walking briskly up to Mr. Moody's verandah.

"Mr. Moody," he cried, extending his hand. "I have come to say goodbye. I am leaving for the west."

Mr. Moody laid his hand on his shoulder, and again spoke to him, urging the claims of Christ. The young man became angry and, shaking off the hand of the evangelist, he replied:

"Mr. Moody, never speak to me again about my soul's salvation. I have promised you to make the decision when I have returned, but not before. Goodbye."

With that he left, and Mr. Moody, realizing that

something had snapped in his own heart, sat down, disappointed.

That night Mr. Moody was awakened by a loud knocking on his door. Putting his head out of the window, he saw a woman with a shawl wrapped around her.

"Oh, Mr. Moody," she cried, her voice filled with anguish, "come quickly. My husband is sick, desperately sick, and I am afraid. Please come at once."

In a moment, Mr. Moody recognized her as the wife of the young man he had spoken to that afternoon.

"It would be no use," was his reply. "Your husband gave me his final refusal this afternoon. He has crossed the deadline. It would be useless for me to go." But because of her entreaties, he got dressed and went.

As he mounted the steps he saw the young man lying on his back on the bed, his eyes wide open, but apparently unconscious of those around him. As he approached he heard him uttering just two words, "Too late! Too late!"

Kneeling down by his side, he grasped his hand, opened his Bible and commenced to pray. But the young man paid no attention whatever. He just kept staring up at the ceiling, and crying out, "Too late! too late! too late!"

Mr. Moody did everything possible to arouse him, but there was no recognition, and in a few minutes he expired, still exclaiming as he had before, "Too late!"

My friend, you may not yet have committed the unpardonable sin. For you it may not yet be too late, but I warn you of the danger of continually rejecting God's offer of mercy. The Spirit may cease to strive, and if He does, you will never have another opportunity.

This, therefore could be your last opportunity. Oh that you would heed the warning, and right now, before it is forever too late, receive Jesus Christ as your own personal Saviour. Will you do it? Do it and do it—NOW!

CHAPTER XI

THE GREATEST STORY EVER TOLD!

MANY years ago an African chief visited Queen Victoria in England. When he was leaving he asked her a question. "Your Majesty," he inquired, "what is the secret of England's greatness?" "The Bible," was the immediate response of the Queen.

The Bible is the greatest Book in the world. No man is educated until he knows it. I have read it every day of my life for over fifty years, and I am going to read it every day until I see my Saviour face to face. I would urge you to do the same.

This Book means more to me than any other book. It is my meat and my drink. The more I study it, the more I love it. There is no other like it. It is God's Book. When I read it God speaks to me. I hear His voice. By it men are saved. By it men live. And by it men are going to be judged. It is our one and only authority. This Book will keep you from sin, or sin will keep you from this Book.

Now the greatest book in the Bible is the Gospel of John. And the greatest chapter in John's Gospel is the third. The greatest verse in the third chapter is the sixteenth. And this is what it says: "For God so loved the world, that He gave His only begotten Son, that whosoever believeth in Him should not perish, but have everlasting life." That is the greatest story ever told.

This, my friends, is the heart of the Gospel. More souls have been saved through John 3: 16 than through any other verse. It is the best-known verse in the Bible and it has been translated into more languages than any other. It is the greatest statement concerning the love of God on record. Moreover it is God's Word.

About a thousand years ago now, a Jewish song-writer, Meir Ben-Isaac Nehoric, wrote a stanza about the love of God, which was later published in *A Book of Jewish Thoughts,* compiled by Joseph Herman Hertz, Chief Rabbi of the British Empire. But no one ever heard of it until one day it was found pencilled on the wall of an insane asylum by an inmate who had died. How he had found it no one will ever know. In my mind it is the greatest poem on the love of God ever written. Here it is:

Could we with ink the ocean fill,
And were the skies of parchment made;
Were ev'ry stalk on earth a quill,
And ev'ry man a scribe by trade;
To write the love of God above
Would drain the ocean dry;
Nor could the scroll contain the whole,
Though stretched from sky to sky.

In John 3: 16, we have four tremendous statements regarding the love of God.

First—"For God so Loved the World"

"For *God* so loved . . ." Salvation starts with God. You had nothing to do with it. Before you were born God provided it for you. Don't think you can discover God. You never can. God is revealed, not discovered. He took the first step.

"For God *so* loved . . ." That little word "so" speaks volumes. It explains all that follows, all that Christ endured for you, all that God suffered when He gave Christ. All He saves you from and all that He provides for you is because He *so* loved you.

"For God so *loved* . . ." The gods of the heathen are gods of hate and fear. Our God is a God of love. The heathen are afraid of their gods. We love our God. Their gods are gods of judgment, power and cruelty bent on doing them injury. Our God is a God of judgment and power also, but first and foremost He is a God of love, seeking to do us good.

God does not love man's sin, but He loves man. You do not love your child's disease but you love your child. Such love as God's is unfathomable. It is a love that cannot be understood, but a love that is real nevertheless. I want you, my friend, to know that God loves you. He loves you no matter what you have done, no matter how great your sin, and He always will love you in spite of your attitude towards Him.

"For God so loved the *World* . . ." That is what makes it impossible for the human mind to comprehend the love of God. The world is made up of rebels, men who have turned their backs on God. Yet, in spite of their rebellion God loved them. The Bible says that "God commendeth His love towards us in that while we were yet sinners, Christ died for us" (Rom. 5: 8); and again it says "Christ died for the ungodly" (Rom. 5: 6). God loved not alone the good but the bad. When Jesus was being nailed to the cross, He prayed, "Father, forgive them; for they know not what they do" (Luke 23: 34). Such love is not human; it is divine. In spite of your enmity, God loves you. What marvellous, matchless love!

Had God wiped out the race as He destroyed the Antediluvians by the flood, and Sodom and Gomorrah by fire, we could have understood it, for that is what man would have done. We did not forgive the Nazi leaders of Germany and give them another chance; we executed them. The Communists of China and Korea cruelly tortured their victims in a most revolting manner. Such is man's inhumanity to man. That is the way man acts. But not so God. His love forgives. God is merciful. He loves the unlovely, the rebellious and the sinful. Such love is supernatural. Only God loves like that.

Had He loved only the lovely the good and obedient, we could have understood it, for we love those who love us. We love our friends; that is human love. But God loves His enemies. He loves the disobedient and sinful. That love we cannot understand. It is beyond our comprehension.

The prodigal's father, you remember, loved his erring son, even though he disgraced him by his life of debauchery and sin. He was waiting with outstretched arms to receive him. "This my son was dead and is alive again," he cried. "He was lost, and is found" (Luke 15: 24). What a welcome! Such is the love of God.

Second—"That He Gave His Only Begotten Son"

"For God so loved the world that He *gave* . . ." Love demands sacrifice. Love produces action. Love must demonstrate itself. That is true even of human love. God has proved His love by giving.

"For God so loved the world that He gave His only begotten *Son* . . ." He could have sent an angel or even an archangel, but He didn't. He sent His Son, His nearest and His dearest. Nothing could have demonstrated His love like the giving of His only begotten Son. A father will give everything he possesses before he will give his son.

Bear in mind, if you will, that God could have rescued His Son even from the cross, and yet He let Him suffer and never raised a hand to save Him. Would you have done that? Could you, as a father, have let your son suffer such excruciating agony, knowing full well that you had the power to rescue him, to save him from it all, and yet never make an effort to do anything? Impossible! There isn't a father in the world who could stand by and see wicked men drive cruel spikes into the hands and feet of his son and not make an effort to save him.

But God did. God allowed His Son to die when He could have rescued Him. That is what makes His love so wonderful. It is a love beyond human understanding. It is not human; it is divine. God's love is so great that He could allow His son to suffer and die and make no effort to save Him, when He could have done so at any time. Such love, I say, is beyond human comprehension. He did it because of His love for you. To save you He had to let His Son die.

Isaac, you remember, was saved, for just as Abraham was about to slay him God cried out, "Abraham, Abraham, lay not thine hand upon the lad" (Gen. 22: 12). But when Jesus, in the agony of His soul, exclaimed, "My God, my God, why hast Thou forsaken me?" (Matt. 27: 46), there was no voice that answered. God turned away His face and let Him die. To save you He had to sacrifice His Son. Oh, what love!

Third—"That Whosoever Believeth in Him"

Now there are three great things in this statement expressed by three words.

First, *whosoever*. Here we have the universality of God's offer of salvation. It is for you, for me, or for anybody else. It takes in the yellow and the brown, the black and the white. It includes sinners of the deepest dye, as well as those who have lived moral and upright lives. It makes no difference what a man is or what he has done, he is included in God's *whosoever*.

Peter thought it was only for the Jews, and God had to give him a special vision before he would go to the Gentiles. God's love is universal, and so is His salvation. It is for Jew and Gentile alike.

I urge you then, to come to Him. You need not fear, no matter what you have done or who you are. God offers you salvation just like anybody else. Drunkards, adulterers, murderers, harlots, liars, thieves, dope-fiends, blasphemers—all may come. God says, *whosoever*.

The second word is the word *believeth*. "Whosoever *believeth* in Him." Faith connects the sinner with God. It simply means trusting Jesus Christ. In other words, you must lean your whole weight on Him. It is a word of action. It has nothing whatever to do with your intellect. It does not say that you must believe certain things about Jesus Christ; it says you must receive Him. "Put your trust in the Lord Jesus, and you will be saved."

You must trust Him as you trust an elevator when you step into it; as you trust a boat when you go aboard; as you trust a train when you enter it. Forget your intellect. Never mind what you believe or what you do not believe. Dare to venture all on Jesus Christ; that is trust. You have believed all your life, now you must act, and when you do you will be saved.

It is "not of works" (Eph. 2: 9). There is nothing you can do to merit it. All your prayers and fastings will not save you. All your churchgoing and religious practices will be unavailing. Penance, self-denial, bodily afflictions, pilgrimages—works of any kind—all, yea, all, will be ineffective. For you are saved, not by works, but by faith.

The third word is the word *Him*, referring, of course, to the Lord Jesus Christ. "Whosoever believeth in Him." Do not worry about your faith. It makes no difference whether you have much or little, nor what kind of faith it is. It may only be like a grain of mustard seed. Forget your faith. Think now of the Object of your faith. Think of the One you are to trust. Put your faith in a person and let that person be the Lord Jesus Christ. It is not your *faith* that saves you; it is Christ.

If you put your faith in the wrong person you will never be saved. If you put your faith in religion or in the church you will not be saved. If you put it in your good works, your morality, again, you will not be saved; but if you put it in Christ He will save you. "Put your trust in the Lord Jesus, and you will be saved" (Acts 16: 31, N.E.B.).

Fourth—"Should not Perish but have Everlasting Life"

There are two things here. First, we are saved from something—"should not perish". We are saved from death. Second, we are given something—"but have everlasting life". We are given Life.

To perish means to die, and to die eternally means to be forever separated from God. That is spiritual death. According to God's word, men are "dead in trespasses and in sins" (Eph. 3: 1), and they have to be quickened into life. Jesus says, "Ye shall die in your sins" (John 8: 24). In other words, unless you receive eternal life you will pass out of this life as you are, namely, "dead in trespasses and in sins".

Look at this fruit. See these vegetables. They all look good. But they are perishing. They are in a state of death. Soon they will become corrupt. Little by little they will rot away. As a matter of fact, they are dead already, for they have been severed from the tree and from the vine. So it is with you. Appearances do not matter. You are already dead; you are right now perishing. Eternal death will be your doom. There is no hope; you cannot be saved—unless you are quickened into life, unless you are grafted into God.

Now God wants to save you from death, and so He offers you life, everlasting life. And I come to you today as His ambassador, with His message of life, eternal life. I offer you now God-life, uncreated life, the life of the ages. Will you have it? Do you want to remain in a state of death? Or do you want this glorious, indestructible Life that God now offers you? It is for you to decide.

This, my friend, is the love of God. Is it not wonderful? What matchless grace! What a glorious revelation! How can you spurn it? How can you turn away? What will you say when you stand before Him? He can forgive anything. But to despise His love, to spurn His offer of mercy, to reject His only begotten Son—that is something that never can be forgiven.

I plead with you because God loves you. This one verse alone is sufficient to prove it. Herein is the Gospel. It is now for you to open your heart and receive the Lord Jesus Christ as your own personal Saviour. "For God so loved the world, that He gave His only begotten Son, that whosoever believeth in Him should not perish, but have everlasting life." This is the greatest story ever told.

"Can You Tell Me the Way to Heaven?"

Let me tell you a story. I read it in a tract. It is rather long, so I am going to condense it for you.

It was during the First World War. Shells were bursting all around. Presently there was a black cloud as pieces of shrapnel came whizzing past. Poor Bert fell like a log. Tiny Tim (6 ft. 3 ins.) jumped down beside him and then returned to his place in the trench.

Suddenly there was a startled cry, "Can you tell me the way to Heaven?" Tiny jumped down again. "The way to Heaven? I'm sorry, chum, I don't know the way, but I'll ask the other fellows."

He returned to the fire-step and walked along to the next man and asked him, but he did not know. So he went on to the man beyond him, but he did not know either. Jumping down, he walked around the trench into the next fire-bay, jumped up on the fire-step and inquired of the third man. Then he went from one to another until he had asked seven men the same question, but none of them knew the way to Heaven.

Leaving that part of the trench, he went on to the next.

His question was always the same, "Bert is dying. He wants to know the way to Heaven. Can you tell him the way?" He had now asked sixteen men, but not one of them could answer his question.

Finally Tiny Tim reached a machine-gunner sitting alone with his gun, his eyes glued on the German lines. The gunner felt a thump on his back and then heard a voice shouting, "Gunner, there is a chap in our company who has been hit. He's dying and he wants to know the way to Heaven. Can you tell him the way?"

The machine-gunner turned around and a smile lit up his face as he replied. "Yes," he said, "I know the way, but I cannot get along the trench. I dare not leave my gun. But wait." Thrusting his hand into his pocket he pulled out a little Testament. Quickly turning over the pages, he said, "Look here, chum, this is the way to Heaven, that verse there, John 3: 16. I'll turn the leaves back, you put your thumb on that verse, and tell him that is the way to Heaven."

Quickly Tiny Tim rushed back. He jumped down beside Bert, who lay so still that for a moment he thought he had gone. He touched his shoulder. "I've got it, Bert," he exclaimed. "Here it is, the way to Heaven, John 3: 16, 'For God so loved the world, that He gave His only begotten Son, that whosoever believeth in Him should not perish, but have everlasting life'."

Poor Bert's eyes were wide open now. He was drinking in every word. What a scene it was—Tiny Tim kneeling on the bottom of the trench, his great hand holding the little Testament, the tears running down his cheeks reading again and again those life-giving words in the ears of Bert.

A look of peace came over the face of the dying man as he kept gasping out "whosoever". After a bit he lay quiet and still again. Tiny Tim got back on the firing step. All at once he called out, "Look, chaps!" And there was Bert. With one last great effort he raised himself up.

He seemed to be gazing at the little piece of blue sky just visible from the trench. His hands were stretched toward it. His face lit up with angelic glory, and with one last gasp, "whosoever", he fell back dead.

Yes, Bert had found the way to Heaven. What a change! One moment in a trench on the battlefield, the next with Christ. What about you? Have you, too, found the way? If not, read the verse again. It is the greatest verse in the Bible. Then open your heart to the Lord Jesus Christ and accept Him as your own personal Saviour. Will you do it? Do it and do it—NOW.